# BRITISH BUSES 1967

# BRITISH
# BUSES
# 1967

## JIM BLAKE

PEN & SWORD
**TRANSPORT**

First published in Great Britain in 2015 by
**Pen & Sword Transport**

An imprint of Pen & Sword Books Ltd
47 Church Street, Barnsley South Yorkshire S70 2AS

ISBN 978 1 47382 717 2

Pen & Sword Books Ltd incorporates the imprints of Pen & Sword Archaeology, Atlas, Aviation, Battleground, Discovery, Family History, History, Maritime, Military, Naval, Politics, Railways, Select, Social History, Transport, True Crime, and Claymore Press, Frontline Books, Leo Cooper, Praetorian Press, Remember When, Seaforth Publishing and Wharncliffe.

For a complete list of Pen & Sword titles please contact
Pen & Sword Books Limited
47 Church Street, Barnsley, South Yorkshire, S70 2AS, England
E-mail: enquiries@pen-and-sword.co.uk
Website: www.pen-and-sword.co.uk

Printed and bound by Replika Press Pvt. Ltd.

# CONTENTS

# ABOUT THE AUTHOR

Jim Blake was born at the end of 1947, just five days before the 'Big Four' railway companies, and many bus companies – including London Transport – were nationalised by Clement Attlee's Labour government.

Like most young lads born in the early postwar years, he soon developed a passionate interest in railways, in particular the steam locomotives still running on Britain's railways in those days. However, because his home in Canonbury Avenue, Islington was just a few minutes walk from North London's last two tram routes, the 33 in Essex Road and the 35 in Holloway Road and Upper Street, Jim's parents often took him on these for outings to the South Bank, particularly to the Festival of Britain which was held there in the last summer they ran, in 1951. Moreover, Jim's father worked at the GPO's West Central District Office in Holborn and often travelled to and from work on the 35 tram. As a result, he knew many of the tram crews, who would let Jim stand by the driver at the front of the trams as they travelled through the Kingsway Tram Subway. This was an unforgettable experience for a 4 year old. In addition, Jim's home was in the heart of North London's trolleybus system, with route 611 actually passing his home, and one of the busiest and complicated trolleybus junctions in the world, at Holloway, *Nag's Head,* a short ride away along Holloway Road. Here, the trolleybuses' overhead almost blotted out the sky. Thus from a very early age, Jim developed an equal interest in buses and trolleybuses to that in railways, and has retained both until the present day.

Jim was educated at his local Highbury County Grammar School, and later at Kingsway College, by coincidence a stone's throw from the old tram subway. He was first given a camera for his fourteenth birthday at the end of 1961, which was immediately put to good use photographing the last London trolleybuses in north-west London on their very snowy last day a week later. Three years later, he started work as an administrator for the then London County Council (LCC) at County Hall, by coincidence adjacent to the former Festival of Britain site, and travelled to and from work on bus routes 171 or 172, which had replaced the 33 and 35 trams mentioned above.

By now, Jim's interest in buses and trolleybuses had expanded to include those of other operators, and he travelled throughout England and Wales between 1961 and 1968 in pursuit of them, being able to afford to travel further afield after starting work. He also purchased a colour cine-camera in 1965, with which he was able to capture what is now very rare footage of long-lost buses, trolleybuses and steam locomotives. Where the latter are concerned, he was one of the initial purchasers of the unique British Railways Standard Class 8 Pacific No 71000 *Duke of Gloucester,* which was the last ever passenger-express locomotive built for use in Britain.

Other preservationists laughed at the group which purchased, what in effect was, a cannibalised hulk from Barry scrapyard at the end of 1973: but they 'laughed on the other side of their faces' when, after extensive and innovative rebuilding, it steamed again in 1986. It has since become one of the best-known and loved preserved British steam locomotives, often returning to the main lines.

Although Jim spent thirty-five years in local government administration, with the LCC's successor, the Greater London Council (GLC), then Haringey Council and finally, literally back on his old doorstep, with Islington Council, Jim also took a break from office drudgery in 1974/75 and actually worked on the buses as a conductor at London Transport's Clapton Garage, on local routes 22, 38 and 253. Working on the latter, a former tram and trolleybus route, in particular was an unforgettable experience. He was recommended for promotion as an inspector, but rightly thought that taking such a job with the surname Blake was unwise in view of the then-current character of the same name and occupation in the *On the Buses* TV series and films, and so declined the offer and returned to County Hall.

By this time, Jim had begun to have his transport photographs published in various books and magazines featuring buses and railways, and also started off the North London Transport Society, which catered for enthusiasts interested in both subjects. In conjunction with this group, he has also compiled and published a number of books on the subject since 1977, featuring many of the 100,000 or so transport photographs he has taken over the years.

Also through the North London Transport Society, Jim became involved in setting up and organising various events for transport enthusiasts in 1980, notably the North Weald Bus Rally which the group took over in 1984, and has raised thousands of pounds for charity ever since. These events are still going strong today.

In addition to his interest in public transport, Jim also has an interest in the popular music of the late 1950s and early 1960s, in particular that of the eccentric independent record producer, songwriter and manager Joe Meek, in whose tiny studio above a shop in Holloway Road (not far from the famous trolleybus junction) he wrote and produced *Telstar* by The Tornados, which became the first British pop record to make No.1 in the USA at the end of 1962, long before The Beatles had even been heard of over there.

When Joe died in February 1967, Jim set up an appreciation society for his music, which has a very distinctive sound.

The society is also still going strong today.

Jim also enjoys a pint or two (and usually more) of real ale, and has two grown-up daughters and three grandchildren at the time of writing. He still lives in North London, having moved to his present home in Palmers Green in 1982.

# INTRODUCTION

Over the past thirty-five years, I have written several books on London's buses and railways, featuring selections from the 100,000 or so transport photographs I took between 1961 and 2014. In recent times, several people have asked me if I have photographs of buses outside London. Indeed I have, since until 1968 my interest in 'provincial' bus, coach and trolleybus fleets equalled that in London Transport (LT), and I travelled widely throughout England and Wales photographing them.

Therefore I am pleased to present a selection of these here, taken in the year 1967. They recall the days when it was possible to travel by train to the Midlands on a Sunday for about thirty bob (£1.50 in today's money) on a cheap day return, or, after the electrification of the West Coast Main Line, for fifty shillings (£2.50) to Liverpool or Manchester. I was able to combine visiting the various bus operators with British Railways' fast disappearing steam engine sheds, too.

In this book, for example, there are several photographs I took in Hampshire, Wiltshire and Dorset when travelling by steam train from Waterloo. Also very useful in the mid/late 1960s were the coach trips organised by the Omnibus Touring Circle (OTC), an offshoot of the PSV Circle, which went for the day to various bus and coach operators, whose depots were visited and whose vehicles were driven out for us to photograph. The highlight of the OTC's year was always a weekend trip to Blackpool at the time of the illuminations in the autumn, visiting interesting operators on the way there and back again.

Sadly, my interest in provincial operators began to wane in 1967, by which time many of the interesting older vehicles had been replaced by such standardised types as the Leyland Atlantean, Daimler Fleetline and, of course, Bristol/ECW types. Trolleybuses – always my favourite mode of road transport – were fast disappearing, too, as were steam locomotives on British Railways. And when, in 1968, London Transport began their ill-fated 'Reshaping Programme', I decided from then on to concentrate only on that operator, which was of course my local one. Unfortunately, I also disposed of most of my photographs and books (notably Ian Allan's British Bus Fleets booklets [BBF]) concerning non-London fleets. It was not until London Routemasters began to be sold to provincial fleets nearly twenty years later that I visited them again.

Therefore I must apologise if some of the details given for the vehicles illustrated herein are a little hazy. Some are from memory, but others I have been able to glean from various websites, and from such 'BBFs' as I have able to re-acquire in recent years.

Except for some of the colour photographs included herein, few of the images in this book have never previously been published. A few London Transport images are also included, and are contemporary to the provincial ones. They are not intended as a complete representation of Britain's buses in 1967 but will, I hope, convey something of cross-section of the total.

Apart from the buses and coaches described in this book, it is perhaps worth putting them all into the context of the world at large in the year 1967. In Britain, Harold Wilson's Labour government had been in power since October 1964, and following its optimistic start after ending what they called 'thirteen years of Tory misrule', was widely seen as beginning to totter. Much in-fighting went on between Wilson's senior ministers, not least involving his deputy, the dipsomaniac George Brown. The economic situation went from bad to worse, culminating in the devaluation of the Pound towards the end of the year, despite Wilson's frequent promises that he would never allow such a thing. On the other hand, Harold Wilson managed to keep Britain out of the disastrous Vietnam War, which was still raging at the time, in spite of relying heavily on 'American' economic help. Indeed, it could be said that Britain finally ceased to be a major world power in 1967, with most British troops being withdrawn 'east of Suez' (notably from Aden) during the year.

Back at home, it was 'the summer of love' with all the trappings of psychedelia and the 'hippy' craze, and although the Beatles were still at the top, their manager Brian Epstein died of an apparent drugs overdose in August 1967. A lesser-known, but equally important, British pop music manager and producer also perished in 1967. This was Joe Meek, whose production and composition *Telstar* by The Tornados band had topped the US record charts at the end of 1962, the first British pop record ever to do so: long before most people, even in Britain, had heard of the Beatles. Joe was also Britain's first independent pop producer, turning out major hit records from his flat above a shop in Holloway Road between 1961 and 1966. He killed himself on 3 February 1967, the eighth anniversary of the death of his idol, Buddy Holly. One iconic British hit record from 1967 was The Kinks' *Waterloo Sunset* and was it just coincidence, I wonder, that it was in the Top Five when the last steamhauled passenger trains ran in the London area, from Waterloo to Bournemouth, Southampton and Weymouth, on 9 July 1967? I suspect not.

After that, steam locomotives survived only in the northwest, apart from a few in the Sunderland area, and all were gone by August 1968. Beyond our shores, the Cold War was at its height, and many people lived in fear of the nuclear holocaust. I did not, however, and as a young lad who was exactly 20 years old as 1967 ended, I was far more interested in continuing my hobby of pursuing buses, coaches, trolleybuses and railway locomotives around the country than worrying whether I would have a future or not.

The photographs in this book are just a fraction of the 4,000 or so I took of them in 1967, and although intended to show just the buses, coaches and trolleybuses themselves, many show other longlost scenes exemplifying life in the Sixties: other road traffic, the fashions of the time, the advertisements on the buses (notably for cigarettes) and also various buildings that no longer exist today. Not least amongst the latter are the various bus and trolleybus depots I visited, particularly in London when many were closed and LT itself no longer existed by then, abolished the Thatcher regime and their sites sold off to eager property developers in the 1980s and early 1990s.

I hope readers will find the selection of pictures entertaining and different – and there are lots, lots more where these came from. Although this book will primarily be of interest to bus enthusiasts, I have tried to make it also of interest to the 'layman' and I hope that the pictures in it also convey some of the atmosphere of what life was like in Britain in 1967 – almost fifty years ago.

Special thanks go to my old friends Paul Everett and Ken Wright for their help in reminding me of the various chassis and body makes and types of the non-London Transport buses and coaches illustrated herein. It is most appropriate that they have done so, for they were actually with me back in 1967 when many of the pictures were taken.

I must also acknowledge the National Trolleybus Association's website for its invaluable help in reminding me of the details of the various trolleybuses which appear in this book. I also must put on record my thanks to the PSV Circle, whose various detailed records of even the most obscure buses and coaches have proved invaluable in my being able to describe them.

My thanks also go to Colin Clarke, who has been painstakingly scanning my 100,000 negatives over the past four years or so, and John Scott- Morgan of Pen & Sword Books for all their help in making this book possible.

*Jim Blake, Palmers Green, 5 April 2014*

*Part One*

# A BRIEF OVERVIEW

**This very rare** 1954 58-seat Crossley-bodied Foden PVD6 double-decker is No.104, one of three built that year for the Warrington Corporation fleet. Foden were based at nearby Sandbach, Cheshire. The firm was better known for building lorries.

**By 1967, only** a few of the once-numerous British municipal trolleybus systems were still operating, and the spring of that year saw two of them close within six weeks! Wolverhampton's trolleybuses perished on 5 March, as will be seen later, whilst those in Maidstone did so on 15 April. Of their normal working, a 1946 Northern Counties-bodied Sunbeam trolleybus No.64 (HKR 3) is seen in the town centre. It had been new to the corporation and, unlike some of its fellows which received new bodies as recently as 1960, still retains its original body. The corporation's coat of arms may be seen on the side of the trolleybus, which is in their traditional livery of light brown and cream. The new replacing buses carried a different scheme of light blue and cream. Note the 'dolly bird' spring fashions displayed in the shop windows on the right, in stark contrast to the doomed trolleybus, dating from the early post-war austerity years. Also, behind the trolleybus may be seen the premises of the Westminster Bank, several years before this was combined with the National Provincial Bank to become 'NatWest'.

## OPERATIONS

As 1967 began the operation of Britain's buses, coaches and trolleybuses was divided into five clear-cut sections.

First of all, many cities and major towns, as well as a few small municipalities, had their own bus fleets, controlled by the local authority. These generally ran services within and just around the city or town boundaries, and ranged from such major conurbations as Birmingham, Glasgow or Manchester, whose fleets numbered several thousand buses, to tiny urban districts like Bedwas and Machen in South Wales, who operated just a handful.

Many municipal fleets had originally begun as tramway systems, most of which converted to trolleybus operation in the inter-war years. In turn, by 1967, trolleybuses were themselves being replaced by motor-buses and only a few systems remained, for example Bradford, Bournemouth, Cardiff, Derby, Huddersfield, Maidstone, Reading, Teesside, Walsall and Wolverhampton. All would be gone within five years.

Most municipal bus fleets sported ornate liveries in varying colour schemes, usually

**In South Wales,** Newport Corporation had a variety of unusual buses in 1967. One was their No.38 (JDW 90), the only Dennis Falcon in their fleet. Seen in a damplooking Newport bus station on 8 April 1967, it dates only from 1954, despite its appearance, and has bodywork by local firm D.J. Davies of Tredegar, constructed on Park Royal frames. Seating only thirty-eight passengers, it nevertheless had a conductor on board.

incorporating the town and city councils' coats of arms, and they also had an excellent variety of vehicle types, ranging from A.E.C.'s, Bristols, Crossleys and Daimlers to Dennises, Guys and Leylands, all with an even greater variety of body makes and styles. Some of

these municipal fleets still operated buses built by long-defunct chassis and body manufacturers in 1967.

Although many single-deck buses had been one-man operated for several years, all double-deckers were still worked with a crew

**Midland Red, or** to be more precise, the Birmingham & Midland Motor Omnibus Company (BMMO) as it was officially named, was one of the largest BET fleets and had one of the most drab liveries of the entire federation – allover red. By 1967, this operator had begun to purchase rear-engined Daimler Fleetlines, with very attractive Alexander bodywork as seen by No. 5410 (GHA 410D), seen in Coventry's Pool Meadow bus station. Dating from 1966, it contrasts with two BMMO single-deckers behind, both of which were built by the operator. The Midland Red bus stop flag next to the Fleetline is also of note, once a common sight in their extensive operating area, which stretched from Worcestershire across the Midlands to Leicestershire.

**At Eastleigh bus** station on 12 March 1967, this splendid Hants & Dorset 1966 Bristol FLF6B Lodekka, with standard Eastern Coachworks bodywork, is No. 1537 (FJD 154D) in their fleet and is bound for Southampton. It will remain in service until 1980, and typifies the vehicles produced for Tilling Group fleets by these two manufacturers throughout the 1950s and 1960s. The first Bristol Lodekkas – so-named because they had low floors and low-height bodies capable of passing beneath low bridges without having to have the hitherto standard arrangement of sunken side gangways on their upper decks, as standard 'low bridge' double-deckers did – first appeared in the early 1950s with rear-entrance bodies. By 1967, only the forward-entrance FLF model as seen here was still being produced. The last were built in 1968. Hants & Dorset's livery was standard Tilling Group green, with cream waistband. As stated on page 15, this group (by then known as the Transport Holding Company) purchased all of the BET fleets in England and Wales in November 1967, and the whole formed the basis of the National Bus Company.

of a driver and conductor, therefore those with rear entrances were still in the majority. By 1967, buses built more than twenty years previously were becoming a rarity with major operators, and those with front entrances and rear engines were rapidly replacing them, and

within a couple of years, new legislation would permit their one-man operation, too. Moreover, from late 1969 onwards, many of the smaller municipal bus fleets, as well as larger ones, would be swallowed up by huge conglomerates such as the West Midlands Public Transport Executive and the South East Lancashire and North East Cheshire P.T.E. Other P.T.E.'s took over both large and small municipal fleets in Merseyside, Teeside, South Yorkshire and West Yorkshire.

Secondly, there were the so-called 'B.E.T.' companies. These were major inter-urban and rural bus and coach operators initially part of the British Electric Transport group, which was affiliated to the 'Big Four' main line railway companies prior to 1948. After that, they were affiliated to British Railways, and therefore semi-nationalised. Such well-known and major operators as Aldershot & District, East Kent, Maidstone & District, Midland Red, Ribble, Southdown, Western Welsh and Yorkshire Traction were included in this group, along with a few smaller fleets, for instance Stratford Blue.

As with the municipal fleets, B.E.T. operators had a rich variety of vehicle liveries

**This Wilts & Dorset** ECW-bodied Bristol MW single-decker, seen at Salisbury bus station on 26 February 1967, typifies those supplied to Tilling Group companies in the late 1950s and the 1960s. This operator had the other standard Tilling Group livery, red with a cream waistband. Other typical Bristol/ECW buses in the Wilts & Dorset fleet are seen on the left, outside their depot, which adjoined the bus station. This bus station was also similar to many others served by these operators, where vehicles arrived at individual bays, and had to reverse to leave the bus station.

– the maroon and cream of East Kent, dark green and cream of Aldershot & District and Maidstone and District and bright green of Southdown being prime examples – as well as ornate fleet names. They had a similar variety of bus and coach chassis types and bodywork, also. A major difference to the municipal fleets was that many of these operators ran express coach services throughout England and Wales, many of which converged on London's Victoria Coach Station.

The wonderful variety of bus and coach types and liveries of the B.E.T. fleets, as with the municipals, was already being eroded by 1967 with standard A.E.C., Daimler or Leyland types ousting earlier vehicles throughout. This would accelerate upon the nationalisation of all B.E.T. fleets in the autumn of 1967 and their inclusion within the new National Bus Company at the beginning of 1969.

The third category of operator as 1967 dawned was the fully nationalised Tilling Group of companies, which had initially been nationalised under the British Transport Commission in the early post-war years. Like the B.E.T. companies, these operated interurban and rural bus services, as well as express coaches throughout the country. Many of the latter worked in association with B.E.T. operators in the 'Associated Motorways' network, whose services not only converged on London, but also Cheltenham. This was still a major transport hub in 1967, before its usefulness as such was lessened by the spread of Britain's motorway system.

Tilling (or 'B.T.C.' fleets as they were still commonly called in 1967) again included major operators such as The Bristol Omnibus Company, Crosville, Eastern Counties, Eastern National, Southern Vectis, United Automobile Services, United Counties, United Welsh and West Yorkshire, as well as smaller fleets like Mansfield District and Midland General. But unlike the B.E.T. fleets, by 1967, they generally presented what, to the transport enthusiast at least, was a boring monotony! Not only did their vehicles virtually all have standardised Bristol chassis and Eastern Coachworks bodies (both manufacturers having already been closely allied to the Tilling Group and then nationalised along with it), which were

**West Riding was** a well-known Yorkshire independent operator, typifying such fleets in various parts of the country. Here, early on Saturday, 7 October 1967, their Roe-bodied Guy Wulfrunian No.953 (VHL 953), dating from 1963, loads up in Bradford. This fleet was one of few to put their faith in this type of bus in the early 1960s, actually being involved with Guy Motors of Wolverhampton in their conception. Virtually all of the 137 Wulfrunians built ended up with them; West Riding had 126 of them from new, and subsequently acquired another six from other fleets. With similar front entrance configuration to Leyland Atlanteans and Daimler Fleetlines, unlike them, these buses did not have a rear engine: it was positioned at the front. To accommodate it, the staircase was positioned on the nearside of the bus, which may be clearly seen by the arrangement of the windows. Despite having standard Gardner engines as fitted to conventional buses of the period, Wulfrunians were notorious for mechanical unreliability, and costs involved in designing and building them, and remedying their faults, contributed to the final demise of Guy Motors in 1969.

usually the only makes Tilling Group fleets were permitted to purchase, and also those manufacturers were forbidden to supply to non-Tilling Group operators, most Tilling Group operators also had a standardised livery, of either red and cream or green and cream!

There were a few exceptions to the standard B.T.C. green or red and cream livery, for instance Midland General's buses, which despite being mainly of Bristol/E.C.W. origin, were blue and cream! This fleet also still had vehicles that were not of that type in 1967, notably a batch of Weymann-bodied A.E.C. Regent III's, some of which will be seen later in this book. Also, in Scotland, although most major rural and inter-urban bus operators were nationalised forming the Scottish Bus Group and also had Bristol/E.C.W. products, very many had A.E.C. or Leyland chassis and bodywork by Alexander of Falkirk. However, towards the end of the 1960's, the regulations restricting Bristol and E.C.W. to supplying vehicles only to Tilling Group fleets was relaxed as was the requirement that those fleets could only buy such products. This eventually led to a greater variety of vehicles, as well as, for example, E.C.W. bodies being fitted to chassis other than Bristol, and vice-versa.

Not surprisingly, the former Tilling/B.T.C. fleets slipped easily into the new National Bus Company framework in 1969, many being merged with former B.E.T. fleets, which had once fiercely competed with them.

The fourth category of bus and coach operator in 1967 was the independent. These fleets had the greatest variety in both the types of vehicle they operated, and the actual scope and size of their operations. There were, for example, the major inter-urban bus and coach operators such as Barton, Lancashire United and West Riding. These generally bought their vehicles new (although Barton was also renowned for a spectacular range of secondhand vehicles) and their services were of similar size to those of comparable B.E.T. or Tilling fleets.

There were also major independent coach companies, which operated express services, tours (including to continental Europe) and private hires, as well as contracts for school or industrial transport. Such names as Grey Green, Wallace Arnold and Yelloway fall into this category.

On the other hand, there were myriad smaller operators, which operated anything from rural and inter-urban stage-carriage services, to school and industrial contracts, private hires, tours and so on. Some of these also bought their vehicles new, for instance

**Grey Green Coaches,** along with their allied Orange Luxury Coaches fleet, under the ownership of the George Ewer Group, was one of the largest and best-known independent coach operators. Based in the North London suburb of Stamford Hill, Grey Green operated a variety of express coach services from London to the east and south coast, even having its own coach stations, for example at Edmonton and Brixton, the latter also being Orange Luxury Coaches' base. They also had extensive touring and private hire interests. Here, at Bressenden Place, Victoria, their 1962 Harrington Cavalier-bodied Leyland Tiger Cub 430EYY has brought a party of theatregoers to town on 18 February 1967: behind is one of their Duple-bodied Bedford coaches. Following the tendering out of London's bus services by the Thatcher regime from 1985 onwards, Grey Green began to operate them, and within fifteen years had evolved into today's Arriva London, which operates a very large share of London's bus services today. Their coastal coach services are now a distant memory.

Delaine of Bourne and South Notts of Gotham, but many acquired larger operators' cast-offs, which often meant that such vehicles lasted far longer with these new operators than they did with their originals. The result was a wonderful variety of bus and coach types and liveries.

Most of these independent fleets survived the ructions caused by the rationalisations of the early 1970s, and, of course, upon the privatisation of the bus industry begun by the Thatcher regime in the 1980s, many still

In 1967, more than half of the 8,000-strong London Transport bus and coach fleet were of the highly standardised post-war RT family, built between 1947 and 1954. Of these, the Leyland versions (RTL class), with Titan PD2 chassis adapted to fit bodies that were mostly interchangeable with the more common AEC Regent III chassis (RT class), were being rapidly withdrawn by 1967. The last of the 500-strong RTW class had been retired from public service in May 1966, although several were retained for driver training, whilst only about a third of the 1,631 RTLs were still in service as 1967 dawned. Earlier in the 1960s, efforts were made to keep newer bodies from these for RTs, which were expected to last longer, and exchange them with older ones from that type. This saw the reappearance of RTLs with bodies carrying front roof route-number blind boxes. Here, one of the twenty-three London Transport RTLs overhauled in 1964/65 with 'roofbox' bodies, Clapton RTL73 (JXN 396), calls at County Hall, my place of employment at the time, on route 170 on 21 August 1967. RTLs at Clapton were imminently due for replacement by RTs at this time. The 170 had replaced Kingsway Subway tram route 31 in 1950, and then been extended to replace trolleybus 555 in 1959, running throughout from Wandsworth to Leyton. When I took this photograph, I could never have guessed that, seven years later, I would take a break from my career in local government administration and work as a conductor at this same garage — though not on route 170. Of note is the statue of the lion, seen behind the RTL. This came from the Lion Brewery on the nearby South Bank. When the brewery, which had been badly bombed during the war, was finally demolished to make way for building the Royal Festival Hall in 1950, the lion was relocated to the approach to Waterloo Station. However when that was redeveloped later in the 1950s, the unfortunate lion 'disappeared' and, when I started work at County Hall just after Christmas 1964, I was surprised to discover it gathering dust in the building's subbasement. Fortunately, the Greater London Council rescued it and placed it on the plinth seen here a few months before this picture was taken, and it remains there today.

**This odd-looking** coach was brand new when seen at Wembley Stadium on 11 March 1967. Belonging to the Red House Motors of Coventry, it is KHP 778E and typifies the unusual types of coach, old and new, to be seen with small independent fleets in the 1960s. With an Albion Viking chassis, it carries a Park Royal 'Royalist' body, built alongside London's Routemasters not very far from Wembley. Only six of these were ever built, four of them going to Red House!

flourish today – but that is another story!

The fifth category is, of course, my local operator, London Transport. Set up as an autonomous organisation in 1933 to operate all bus, tram and trolleybus services in Greater London and in the country areas around it as far out as Hitchin, Brentwood, Sevenoaks, Crawley, Guildford, High Wycombe and Luton, it had been nationalised as the London Transport Executive at the beginning of 1948, then reconstituted as the London Transport Board fifteen years later. Its last trams were replaced by buses in July 1952, and, sadly, its huge trolleybuses system – once the world's largest – was finally abandoned in May 1962. Despite being a nationalised concern, London Transport was not forced to buy Bristol and E.C.W. products as other B.T.C.-controlled concerns were, but allowed to continue its policy of buying mainly A.E.C. but also Leyland chassis, bodied by Park Royal, Metro-Cammell, Weymann, Saunders and, in the case of the 500-strong RTW class, Leyland itself. To many enthusiasts, especially when the

trolleybuses had gone, the fleet was a boring one in 1967, comprising around 4,500 RT-types, all of which had a standardised appearance, most of the 700 RF-class single-deckers, and all but the last few of the 2,760 Routemasters.

Only a handful of non-standard types were in London Transport's fleet in the mid-1960s. These were the low-bridge Weymann-bodied A.E.C. Regent III RLH-class double-deckers, and some small Guy GS-class single-deckers (which did have E.C.W. bodies) which had broken the monotony until late 1965, which was compounded by a standard livery of red with a cream (or, latterly grey) waistband for Central Area buses in Greater London or Lincoln green with a cream waistband for Country Area buses (light green waistband for Green Line coaches). But things then began to change. Rear-engined, front-entrance doubledeckers were bought for trials in both areas in 1965, along with a small batch of modern coaches for Green Line work. Most importantly, the first new rear-engined single-deckers had appeared in early 1966 for the first Central London 'Red Arrow' commuter services, and mass delivery of this type began as 1967 drew to close.

Indeed, 1967 was the last year that London Transport's services would be wholly operated by its traditional bus types (other than about eighty experimental vehicles), as mass introduction of the new vehicles began, after many delays, in September 1968. Things would never be the same again, and on 1 January 1970, London Transport's Country Area and Green Line services were taken away to become part of the new National Bus Company, in the shape of its subsidiary, London Country Bus Services Ltd. Ironically for me, overall control of London Transport's Central Area (red) buses and its Underground railways passed to the Greater London Council, by whom I had been employed by then for almost five years!

## VEHICLE TYPES

Where double-deckers are concerned, as mentioned above, because one-man operation of double-deck buses was not yet allowed, traditional half-cab, rear entrance double-deckers were still being built in 1967. By now, the main bus chassis manufacturers were A.E.C., Bristol, Daimler and Leyland. The latter

two, however, had been producing rear-engined, front entrance doubledeckers for several years, in the form of the Fleetline and Atlantean respectively. These were to be found in both municipal and B.E.T. fleets, and even London Transport had eight Fleetlines and fifty Atlanteans in trial service. Guy Motors were still building buses in 1967, though on their last legs following the failure of their revolutionary Wulfrunian double-decker. Albion, by now a Leyland subsidiary, was also still producing a few vehicles, too. However, half-cab Daimler CVG's and Leyland Titan PD3's were still being built for municipal and B.E.T. fleets. Bristol were still producing their famous Bristol Lodekkas, though by now only the forward-entrance FLF version, for Tilling Group fleets. However, their first rearengined double-deckers, the VR's – at first bodied only by E.C.W. – had begun to appear by 1967, and also would be made available to fleets other than

**On 20 March** 1967, London Transport's XMS7 (JLA 58D) is seen at Victoria Bus Station on their first 'Red Arrow' flat-fare commuter service, which connected this busy terminus with Marble Arch and Oxford Street. Operated with the first six of these Strachan-bodied, rear-engined, dualentrance/ exit AEC Swifts (or Merlins as London Transport preferred to call them), route 500 had been introduced in April 1966, with a flat-fare of sixpence (2$^1$/$_2$p) collected by an automatic device resembling a fruit machine. The forward portion of these buses, which had front entrances and centre exits, was for standing passengers only, leading to their being unkindly nicknamed 'cattle trucks'. A further nine of these experimental buses were intended as conventional one-man-operated Country Area buses, but all but one of them were instead converted to 'Red Arrow' vehicles and painted red, as this one had recently been when seen here. On the right is RTL363, a Leyland working busy trunk route 25 from West Ham Garage, which will be a victim of MB-types upon their mass introduction in September 1968. Just visible on the left is a Routemaster on route 16. This now famous type of London bus will long outlast the 'cattle trucks', all of which had gone by mid-1981, surviving in every day service until the end of 2005, and still on 'heritage' service today.

**Under the trolleybus** wires in Maidstone on 15 March 1967 is East Kent Park Royalbodied AEC Regent V YJG825, dating from 1962, working route 10 to Folkestone, which was jointly operated with fellow BET operator Maidstone & District. East Kent had several batches of identical vehicles, built between 1961 and 1968, as well as an initial batch of forty built in 1959, also bodied by Park Royal, but with full fronts. Some of the Regent Vs survived into the 1980s, by which time East Kent and Maidstone & District had become combined within the National Bus Company 'empire'.

**The yard of** Park Royal Vehicles' factory, flanking the Grand Union Canal, reveals some of London Transport's last standard Routemaster buses awaiting delivery and nearing completion on 4 March 1967. Nearest the camera is RML2599 (NML 599E), first of the final batch, which ended at RML2760. Behind it are two of the sixty-five front-entrance Routemaster coaches built for British European Airways (BEA) during the winter of 1966/67, construction of which caused a temporary cessation of building the standard London Transport examples. These coaches were operated and maintained by LT staff, and most would end up in the LT fleet in the late 1970s. On the right, a single-decker with offside entrances and exits is just visible, perhaps for export to Portugal, where many AEC and Park Royal buses ran – including a couple of the former BEA Routemasters many years later.

**Western Welsh was** a typical B.E.T. operator, whose fleet in 1967 largely consisted of A.E.C.s and Leylands. This singledecker, their No.1206, a Leyland Olympian with Weymann 44-seat bodywork built in 1956, is also typical of those operated by many such fleets, and although suitable for oneman operation, it is quite likely to still have a conductor on board, as many single-deckers did well into the 1970s, since there is no notice on its front advising passengers to 'pay as they enter'. It is seen leaving Cardiff Bus Station on 8 April 1967 bound for the quaintly-named town of Llantwit Major. Note the trolleybus wires visible above it on the left; British Railways' Cardiff General Station forms a nice backdrop. Conveniently, Cardiff's main bus and railway stations are situated next door to each other!

just the Tilling Group. Only A.E.C. was still producing only half-cab double-deckers. These were, firstly, the well-tried Regent Vs, which operators such as East Kent were still buying as late as 1968, as well, of course, as Routemasters for London Transport. Their last 160-odd were built during the year (though the final handful were not actually delivered until early 1968) as were the remainder of the British European Airways examples.

Unfortunately, the rear-engined Routemaster was a dead duck thanks to the policies of Harold Wilson's Transport Minister Barbara Castle, whose department forced London Transport to abandon its policy of having vehicles of its own design built for it, more's the

pity. The sole example entered service in July 1967, as will be seen later on.

## Single-deck buses

By 1967, as the pictures in this book will show, very few half-cab single-deck buses remained in service, having been superseded by underfloor-engined types from the early 1950s onwards. As mentioned earlier, these were usually capable of being one man operated, with their entrance directly adjacent to the driver, although some (for instance London Transport's RF class A.E.C. Regal IV's) still had conductors well into the 1970s. Chassis-wise, A.E.C., Leyland and Bristol had the single-deck bus market virtually to themselves in 1967, and all three had recently begun producing rear-engined types, the Swift, Panther and RE respectively. Bristol's RE-types had been around the longest and were by far the most successful. There were also a few single-deck versions of the rear-engined Daimler Fleetline produced. Lighter, smaller buses were also produced by Bedford and Ford, with chassis types more usually bodied as coaches.

## Coaches

Similarly, A.E.C., Leyland and Bristol led the way in production of coach chassis in 1967, usually with larger and heavier types that operated express services. The market for

**Many single-deck** vehicles in British bus fleets in the 1950s and 1960s were classified as 'dual-purpose', meaning that they could be used as buses on stage carriage services or as coaches on express services. In an effort to modernise its Green Line fleet, London Transport purchased fourteen Willowbrook-bodied AEC Reliance coaches in 1965. These were built to what, in effect, was a standard design for dual-purpose single-deckers, favoured by BET group fleets in particular. They entered service at the end of November that year on route 705 (Sevenoaks to Windsor), whose western section ran limited stop along the M4. They were not a success, and we see here RC2 (CUV 60C) loading up at Hyde Park Corner on their last day on this route, 29 November 1967, just two years after their introduction. After use on other Green Line routes, and a repaint into traditional Lincoln-Green livery, they ended up as London Country buses on route 390 at Hertford and all were withdrawn from service in the mid-1970s.

lighter coaches, used for touring or private hire work, was dominated by Bedford, though Ford with their Thames coaches had become a competitor to them in recent years. The recently-launched and peculiar-looking Park Royal 'Royalist'-bodied Albion Vikings, as seen earlier in these pages, came to nothing. By far the most unusual coaches being built at the time were Bedford VAL's, which were six-wheelers with front, four-wheel twin steering. A few of these were also bodied as single-deck buses.

## Body Makers

A good variety of bus and coach body makers still existed in 1967. As mentioned previously, Eastern Coach Works bodied virtually all Bristol chassis, whilst firms such as Park Royal, Metro-Cammell, Weymann, Roe, Marshall, Northern Counties, Willowbrook and East Lancs built the lion's share of bodies on most other buses, both double- and single-deck. Alexander built most bodies for buses and coaches in Scotland, but was also popular south of the border, notably for bodying many Daimler Fleetlines and Leyland Atlanteans in English and Welsh fleets. Smaller builders such as Strachan and Yeates were still building bodies too, the latter mostly for coaches. Apart from those in the Tilling fleets with their obligatory E.C.W. bodies, most British coaches in 1967 were bodied by either Duple or Plaxton, the graceful bodies built by Harrington had ceased production early in 1966, in effect selling out to Plaxton, whilst Burlingham had become Duple's subsidiary Duple Northern a few years before.

**One of Harrington's** final products was this Grenadier-bodied Leyland Leopard PSU3. Parked in Coventry, JHV 498D is in the fleet of the famous North London independent fleet Grey Green Coaches, and on 19 March 1967 has taken me on an Omnibus Touring Circle trip to various bus and coach operators in Warwickshire. A sad loss to the British coach industry was the closure of Harrington's coachworks in Hove, Sussex, in April 1966.

**Seen awaiting delivery** on 11 March 1967 outside Duple's West Hendon factory, which flanked the Edgware Road, is LUK593E, a Viceroy-bodied Ford 593E destined for the well-known independent operator and commercial vehicle dealer Don Everall of Wolverhampton. This type of coach is typical of those being supplied to independent coach fleets for touring and private hire work in 1967. Duple had originally opened its Hendon factory in 1926. It was enlarged in the 1930s, but finally closed in 1970 when coach building was transferred to their Blackpool factory.

## Part Two

# BUS, COACH AND TROLLEYBUS OPERATORS IN ENGLAND AND WALES, 1967

**Few people in** their right mind would have travelled for the day to Bournemouth on a cold, grey January day, but that is what a friend and I did on Sunday, 15 January 1967! We travelled behind a Bulleid 'Pacific' (No. 34098 *Templecombe*) from Waterloo, and the purpose of our trip was to visit both the engine shed and Bournemouth Corporation's trolleybus depot. Here on that gloomy Sunday is their 1958 Weymann-bodied Sunbeam No.273 at The Square terminus of trolleybus route 21.

**At the Corporation's** Mallard Road Depot itself, 1950 Weymann-bodied B.U.T. 9641T six-wheeler No.254 makes a sad sight dumped out of use amongst several others of this batch. There had been twenty-four of these splendid trolleybuses.

**Hants & Dorset was** the main inter-urban operator serving Bournemouth, and being a Tilling Group fleet, had standardised on Eastern Coach Works Ltd (ECW)-bodied Bristols. On that grey January Sunday, many of their buses were parked out of use in Bournemouth's main bus station. This one, No.1279, is one of six low-bridge Bristol KS6Bs supplied in 1951. It lasted until 1971, after Hants & Dorset absorption into the National Bus Company.

**Sadder still, several** of the 1958 Sunbeam trolleybuses were also out of use, and would remain lined up like this outside the depot until the system was finally abandoned in April 1969. Here, No's 267, 260 and 258 are nearest the camera. In common with most Bournemouth buses and trolleybuses of the period, they had rear open platforms as entrances, and front exits beside the driver's cab, and so could have been adapted for one-man operation. Fortunately, some of this type of trolleybus – the last, dating only from 1962/3, being the last trolleybuses ever built for a British operator – survive in preservation.

**It's hard to** believe now, but Bristol Lodekkas were still being produced for Tilling Group fleets in 1967. On 15 January 1967, brand new Hants & Dorset E.C.W.-bodied FLF6G 1555 lays over in Bournemouth Bus Station. Some of these latecomers had much shorter lives than older Bristol/E.C.W. products, due to the rapid withdrawal of crew-operated buses under the National Bus Company regime in the 1970s. This one, however, survived until 1980, by which time crew-operated buses (i.e. those with a driver and conductor) were rare in Britain, other than in London.

**At this period,** London Transport were experimenting with fifty Park Royal-bodied Leyland Atlanteans, which were their XA class, in comparison with fifty RML-type 30ft-long Routemasters. They were operated on routes 24, 67, 76 and 271 in North London. XA2, second of the class, which for some reason had a cut-away front overhang, calls at York Road, Waterloo on its way to Victoria on the 76 on 24 January 1967. Eight similarly bodied Daimler Fleetlines, the XF class, were also tried, and despite being green, Country Area buses were also tested in the Central Area in comparison with the XAs, eight of which ran in red in the Country Area. Rather unsurprisingly, the RMLs came out on top, and a further 450 were built after the fifty-eight 'trial' buses, most seeing up to forty years at London's service. The XAs, meanwhile, were transferred to suburban one-man-operated routes in South London in 1969/70, but sold to Hong Kong in 1973. The XFs passed to London Country in January 1970, and lasted until 1980/81.

**At this period,** my interest in independent coach fleets equalled that in the major bus and trolleybus fleets, and, as mentioned earlier, these had vehicles with a great variety of body styles and manufacturers. Here in Penton Street, Islington, on 3 February 1967, is Evan Evans Tours 1959 Bedford SB1 WXE 942, which has bodywork by Thurgood of Ware, Herts. Sadly, a few knocks and bumps mar its dark maroon and cream livery.

**Typical of privately** owned touring coaches to be seen in London in 1967 is DDX 413, a 1955 Plaxton-bodied AEC Reliance, working for Goldmsith's Coaches of Sicklesmere, Suffolk. It is seen on 4 February 1967 outside Euston Station, then still in the throes of rebuilding. The building on the left, a typical Leslie Green Underground station, is the original Hampstead tube building, which was taken out of use when Euston underground station was rebuilt to accommodate the new Victoria Line.

**Grey Green 1965** Duple Bella Vega-bodied Bedford SB ELU 510C stands at Finsbury Park, Wells Terrace, on 5 February 1967, working the London Transport Northern City Line replacement service to Drayton Park, necessary owing to that line's tunnels and platforms at Finsbury Park being taken over for the new Victoria Line. At this period, the well-known North London coach operator, Grey Green, ran coastal express services, as well as tours, school contracts and private hires. Their operation of London bus routes twenty years later was unthinkable at this time!

**Across the road** in the British Railways Eastern Region's works yard off Stroud Green Road, early post-war Saunders-bodied Leyland Tiger PS1/1 (KRB 87) was new in 1948 to Midland General, whose blue livery it still carries, as their No.201. It is in use as a staff bus for BR permanent way staff maintaining the East Coast main line, long before privatisation. It had passed to them in December 1962.

**Albert Harling of** Lambeth had contracts with St Thomas's and Westminster Hospitals at this period to provide transport for nurses. Ex-Green Line RF224 (MLL 611), one of a number withdrawn by London Transport in 1964/65, is one of the vehicles used on them, which also included three RFWs (LTs 1951 ECWbodied AEC Regal IV touring coaches) and one of the green RTLs that had worked from Hatfield a few years before. On 7 February 1967, it accompanies a Bedford VAL and SB, both Duple-bodied, in Harling's yard beside the main line out of Waterloo.

**Super Coaches of** Upminster was a well-known independent fleet, and the forerunner of today's successful 'Ensignbus' business. They too worked school contracts and private hires, and had many ex-London Transport buses, including a number of RLHs, Weymann-bodied AEC Regent IIIs. Here, former RLH15 and RLH3, from the 1950 batch of twenty diverted from Midland General, stand outside LTs Manor House offices working the special service from the nearby Piccadilly Line station to Tottenham Hotspur's football ground at White Hart Lane on 11 February 1967.

**One of the** smallest British municipal operators was West Bridgford Urban District Council, whose territory was across the River Trent from Nottingham. Here, in Nottingham on 19 February 1967 is their No.41 (BRR 241C), one of two forward-entrance East Lancs-bodied AEC Renowns supplied to them in 1965. Their livery was brown and cream, and in September 1968, their routes and buses, including this one, were taken over by Nottingham City Transport. With a lower body height than the similar Regent V, the AEC Renown first appeared in 1962, but was never as numerous or successful as the Regents.

**Seen in Midland** General's Alfreton Depot on the same day are two of their 1950 low-bridge Weymann-bodied AEC Regent IIIs, No.423 (ONU 632) and 424 (ONU 633), which are very similar to London Transport's RLH class, of which the first twenty were a diverted order from this operator, as seen with the Super of Upminster examples above. They are flanked by two Bristol Lodekkas. This Tilling Group operator was unusual in having a blue and cream livery, rather than the usual red or green.

**Far from standard** in the Wilts & Dorset fleet is No.901 (PHR 829), a 1957 Harrington-bodied dual-purpose Leyland Tiger Cub single-decker, which had been taken over from the well-known independent operator Silver Star of Porton Down in 1963. The 'peak' above its cab windows was a feature common to most buses and coaches built new for Silver Star, their eponymous emblem having been displayed on it. It makes an interesting contrast with the standard Bristol/ECW products parked nearby in Salisbury bus station on 26 February 1967.

**Another old bus** used by a contractor at this period is NJO 717, a Willowbrook bodied AEC Regal III that had been new to City of Oxford Motor Services as their No.717 in 1950. Seen in Wembley High Road on 4 March 1967 it is with Eagre Construction, who had contracts with British Rail at the time.

**On the same** day as the previous picture, hundreds of coaches converged on Wembley Stadium for a sporting event. One is 1957 centre-entrance Harrington Wayfarer-bodied AEC Reliance SWP 722 belonging to Regent Coaches of Redditch. Wembley was a 'Mecca' for bus and coach enthusiasts at this period, when buses and coaches of all shapes, sizes, makes and ages (well, at least since the 1930s!) could turn up, as well as major operators' cast-offs with independent fleets. I had no interest in the sporting events themselves, unless Arsenal were playing!

**In contrast, new** coaches could be seen there too. Brand new Whittle of Highley HUJ 509E is a Bedford VAM, whose Duple Viceroy body was built at their nearby Hendon factory. It is seen in Empire Way approaching the stadium. The crowds seen on foot have come from Wembley Park Station, then on London Transports Bakerloo and Metropolitan Lines. Both Wembley Stadium, of course, and Wembley Park Station have changed beyond recognition since these pictures were taken, along with the surrounding area.

**Next day, Sunday,** 5 March 1967, was the last day of regular express passenger services from Paddington to Wolverhampton, to where I was able to travel for about thirty bob (£1.50) cheap day return. Wolverhampton had its own municipal bus fleet, and many of the corporation's buses were Guys, the factory of that chassis manufacturer being in the Falling's Park district of the town. Here we see 1950 Park Royal-bodied Guy Arab III No.552, recently withdrawn owing to accident damage. Does the blind really say Batman's Hill?

**Wolverhampton Corporation also** experimented with Guy's ill-fated Wulfrunian, one of which is seen at their Fallings Park Depot. This is East Lancs-bodied No.70, dating from 1961 and one of just two in their fleet. This nearside view clearly shows how the staircase on these strange vehicles was on the nearside, rather than the offside as on other front entrance double-deckers. Although it passed to West Midlands PTE, when that operator took over the Birmingham, Walsall, West Bromwich and Wolverhampton fleets in October 1969, it never carried their livery, and was withdrawn a few months later in 1970.

**By coincidence, Sunday,** 5 March 1967 was also the last day of Wolverhampton Corporation's trolleybuses. Here, their No.452, a 1948 Sunbeam 'W', which had been rebodied by Roe only in 1960, passes the A.B.C. Cinema on route 58 bound for Dudley. Note its bent booms, which somehow blended in with the shabbiness of the town, which at this time also suffered from tensions between the locals and immigrants imported there to work in the local factories, made famous by the local MP (and former Tory cabinet minister) Enoch Powell's notorious but prescient 'Rivers of Blood' speech just over a year later.

**Showing distorted booms,** too, No.449 of the same batch runs in to the depot for the last time. Overhead, the complicated trolleybus can be seen and, to the left, several other photographers are also present to record this sad event.

**The booms of** the same trolleybus are lowered for the last time: this view nicely shows the long pole which was carried beneath many British trolleybuses for such purposes, particularly when they came off the wires at busy junctions! Other trolleybuses had retriever wires attached to their booms and fastened to the rear of their bodies for this purpose.

**Preserved Wolverhampton trolleybus** No.654, one of nine Guy BT's with Park Royal bodywork built in 1950, and in fact the corporation's last new trolleybus, ran on the last day but here stands with its booms down to allow service trolleybuses to pass. Two of these, of the Roe rebodied Sunbeam 'W' batch, are seen behind it.

**Don Everall was** an independent operator in Wolverhampton, and also a dealer in second-hand buses and trucks. This very unusual double-decker is a Strachan-bodied Ford Thames Trader, built in 1963 as London Transport's TT4 for a service ferrying cyclists through the newly opened Dartford Tunnel. The cycles went on open racks on their lower decks, the passengers upstairs, with entrances on both sides of the bus, behind the driver's cab. So few people used the service that it was withdrawn after about eighteen months. Note the 'For Sale' notice in the windscreen. Some hopes!

**It was still** common in the late 1960s for old buses to end up with showmen. Here, also in Wolverhampton on 5 March 1967, pre-war Bristol JO5G single-decker BHN 214, which had originated with United Automobile Services in the North East, is parked up at a showman's winter quarters. It appears to be in use as their living accommodation. The old single-decker had been new as United's BJO19 in 1936, with an Eastern Counties (the forerunner of ECW) body, but given a new body built by Croft in 1946, only to be withdrawn in 1954, when it passed to the showman.

**Bedford OBs, dating** from the early post-war years could still be seen in use in 1967, too. Here we see Duple Vista-bodied BJR 679, with Gilbert's Coaches of Tunbridge Wells who were well known for keeping elderly vehicles in service at the time. It had been new to Armstrong of Westerthorpe in March 1947, thus was exactly 20 years old when seen arriving at Wembley on 11 March 1967, where I had returned for another sporting event that brought a vast array of interesting buses and coaches.

**One of several** real oddities there that day was Suffolk independent operator Norfolk of Nayland's early AEC Regal IV LWT 147, carrying a very rare centre-entrance Whitson coach body. It was new in May 1952 to Yorkshire independent operator Ripponden & District, and contrasts with two more recent Duple-bodied Bedfords parked behind it, at least one of which is a VAL.

**Next day, 12** March 1967, I again travelled by steam train out of Waterloo, this time to Winchester where at the Hillside Garage, Chesil Street, of the famous independent fleet King Alfred, I photographed JOR 594, a 1951 all-Leyland PD2/1, accompanying 1959 Weymann-bodied Leyland Tiger Cub WCG103. This operator sold out to Hants & Dorset (part of the National Bus Company [NBC]) in April 1973. However, on each New Year's Day various of its former buses are used to re-create its operations in and around Winchester, attracting transport enthusiasts from all over the country.

**On Wednesday, 15** March 1967, I went 'sick' from work at County Hall (having used up all my 1966/67 leave entitlement) to travel down to Maidstone, as I had been told trolleybus services were finishing that day. One of them, No.58 (GKP 513) seen here, is a wartime Sunbeam, originally bodied by Park Royal in 1944 and given a new Roe body only in 1960. It is bound for Barming, near the corporation's trolleybus depot. Next day, I was told off for taking too much sick leave, and was then outraged to find the trolleybuses actually finished a month later, and on a Saturday, too – a day when I would not have been at 'work' anyway!'. However, many years later I discovered that the day I went there was the last day of normal trolleybus operation – the runs on the Sunday were special farewell journeys only.

**The main inter-urban** operator in Maidstone was Maidstone & District, whose headquarters were also in the town. Here we see their DH385, a 1951 all-Leyland Titan PD2/12 with a high-bridge body. Though mainly serving the western part of Kent beyond the London Transport area, this operator with its smart dark green and cream-liveried buses, ran joint services to such distant places as Brighton, Canterbury and Folkestone with fellow BET fleets Southdown and East Kent respectively. All three, of course, became part of the National Bus Company in 1969. This vehicle was withdrawn the following year.

**Caught at London** Bridge Station on my way home from Maidstone that day is London Transport's RTL932. This was one of the last three of the 450 Metro-Cammell-bodied examples remaining in service at the time, all were based at Bow Garage for routes 10 and 25. It is of similar vintage and chassis to the Maidstone Leyland PD2 seen above since, of course, London's RTLs had Leyland Titan PD2 chassis modified to carry bodies compatible with the RT class AEC Regents, though to confuse the issue, Metro-Cammell bodies could only be fitted to RTL PD2 chassis anyway.

**The first Omnibus** Touring Circle day trip of the 1967 season took place on Sunday, 19 March, visiting various operators in Warwickshire. This view taken at the depot of independent operator Priory of Leamington shows two of their early post-war all Leyland Titan PD2s JUE358 and JUE 359. They were new to Stratford Blue in 1950, and withdrawn by them in 1964. The gentleman standing two to the left of these wearing the tie is John Kaye, who organised the OTC trips and was also active in the PSV Circle. A number of the other enthusiasts on the trip are also in view – I wonder how many are still around to read this book? My old friends Paul Everett and Ken Wright are, and both helped me compile it.

**Priory Coaches also** had several elderly ex-Coventry Corporation Daimlers, one of these being FHP 3, once Coventry's No.3, a 1948 CVA6 with a Birminghamstyle MCW body. It had been withdrawn by Coventry in 1966, so had recently been acquired by Priory.

**Nearby was another** independent operator, G & G of Leamington, who had another of the same batch of ex-Stratford Blue Leyland Titan PD2s, JUE 355. The railway line alongside the buses, in both this and the picture of the other two ex-Stratford Blue Titans with Priory Coaches, is the former Great Western main line from Paddington to Birmingham, Snow Hill, which had lost its regular express services two weeks before. Today, this line again has a regular express service to and from Marylebone.

**Our next port** of call on this trip was Coventry, where the corporation's MCCW Orionbodied Daimler CVG6 No.264 (VWK 264) sets off from Pool Meadow bus station on route 4 for Wyken. This operator had standardised on Daimler chassis for many years, and this bus was one of a batch of fifty supplied in 1958.

**A brand new** Coventry Corporation bus seen at their depot that day is No.518 (KHP 518E), one of six ECW-bodied Bristol RESL6Gs just supplied to them. Regulations had recently been relaxed allowing Bristol and ECW to supply to non-Tilling Group fleets for the first time in best part of twenty years, but Coventry had only six such vehicles. In common with other recent Coventry vehicles, they would pass to West Midlands PTE in 1974.

**Also at the** depot, a group of 1949 Birmingham-style M.C.C.W.-bodied Daimler CVA6's include No.89, apparently still in service, and No.54, 55 and 56 which have been demoted to training duties. No. 89 was withdrawn later in 1967, though two others of its batch lasted into 1968.

**No.59 of the** same batch of the buses seen in the previous picture is seen inside the depot. It has recently been cut down for use as a tree-lopper, as old double-deckers often were in the 1950s and 1960s, but quite why the more modern tin-front Daimler next to it has been too is a mystery to me – a low bridge accident maybe?

**Between 1961 and** 1967, I spent many Saturdays at London's Victoria Coach Station observing the huge variety of coaches that could be seen there, especially on Bank Holiday weekends. On Easter Saturday, 25 March 1967, Red & White 1953 ECW-bodied Bristol LS6G DS253 is, in fact, an oddity in this fleet despite it being a Tilling Group fleet. Most of the coaches they used on Associated Motorways services from South Wales to London were built by local coachbuilder Lydney in the Forest of Dean prior to then, and in fact only sixteen Bristol LS coaches were supplied to Red & White, though later on they had several more Bristol MW's with similar bodywork! To the right may be seen one of Eastern National's double-deck Bristol Lodekka coaches, also, of course, with ECW bodywork, used on express service X10 between London and Southend.

**Next day, Easter** Sunday, 26 March 1967, I travelled with my old friend, Ken Wright, to Barry Island to visit Dai Woodham's scrap yard, which at the time contained nearly 200 withdrawn steam locomotives, mainly from the Southern and Western Regions of British Railways. We had about half an hour between changing trains at Cardiff, where in the bus station adjacent to what was then BR's Cardiff General Station we find Western Welsh 1961 Weymannbodied Albion Nimbus No.29. Despite Western Welsh having forty-eight of them (twenty-four bodied by Harrington in 1960 and twenty-four by Weymann in 1961), these little buses did not last long here, their routes losing out to motor car competition.

**On the same** day, this group of buses stand in the yard of Western Welsh's Barry Depot: 1956 low-bridge Park Royal-bodied AEC Regent V No.657 accompanies 1953 Weymann-bodied Leyland Tiger Cub No.1005. They typify the buses supplied to English and Welsh BET operators in the 1950s.

**1962 Western Welsh** Weymann lowbridge-bodied Leyland Atlantean No.337 passes the depot, which bizarrely would be used as a store for steam engines rescued from the nearby scrap yard in more recent years! Today, more appropriately, preserved Welsh buses are stored there. Although Atlanteans and the similarly configured Daimler Fleetlines, with their front entrances directly opposite the driver's cab, could have been one-man operated, government legislation did not allow this until more than ten years after their introduction.

**This extremely unusual** coach, BMK 345A, is a Bedford VAL14 six wheel, twin-steerer new in 1963 to Rowson's Embassy Coaches of Hayes, working for Evan Evans tours. The ungainly looking body, however, was new to one of the VAL prototypes, exhibited at the 1962 Commerical Motor Show, and then transferred to this VAL chassis in July 1963. It is the only Weymann Topaz body ever built, and was therefore unique. This view finds it in the coach park opposite Westminster Abbey on Easter Monday, 27 March 1967, by which time it had acquired a Duple front grille.

**A more traditional** coach seen on the same day is East Kent HJG 28, a Duple Britannia centre-entrance Dennis Lancet UF built in 1954. Although built for touring, including on the continent, these coaches often worked East Kent's express services to London at busy times, as this one is doing when arriving at Victoria Coach Station on Easter Monday. East Kent had favoured Dennis for their single-deck bus and coach fleets for many years, and when production of the Lancet UF ceased later in the 1950s, they turned to AEC instead.

**On Saturday,** 1 April 1967, Battersea-based RTL22 (JXN 342) passes The Stanley Arms, Chelsea on its way from Putney Common to Homerton on eponymous route 22. When I took this photograph, I had no idea that some seven or eight years later, I would be working as a conductor on this route. Back in 1967, this was the lowest-numbered London Transport RTL still in service as most other lownumbered ones had been sold in 1958/59. It was withdrawn a few days after this was taken, replaced by RTs being drafted in to replace RTLs at Battersea: a few weeks after that route 22 converted to RM operation.

**Also on** 1 April 1967, Park Royal-bodied AEC Regal IV MLL732 is seen at the former Chiswick tram depot, where coaches operated by British European Airways on express services from Earls Court to London Heathrow Airport had recently been transferred. These half-deck vehicles had large luggage boots at the rear, and were operated and maintained by London Transport. They were classified as 4RF4, the chassis being the same as LT's own 700-strong RF class. At the time this was taken, they were being replaced by new-forward entrance Routemasters, which eventually became LT's RMA class. One of these is visible on the right, complete with its luggage trailer.

**Next day, Sunday,** 2 April 1967, I went on a day trip by train from St Pancras to Derby, and by the time we got there, it was pouring with rain. We carried on regardless, and here heading out of town alongside British Railways' famous Derby Works is Derby Corporation's 1952 Willowbrook-bodied Sunbeam F4 trolleybus No.223. It is on route 41 bound for Alvaston. Expansion of the trolleybus system further out from the town centre in the mid-1950s was thwarted by locals not wanting the picturesque countryside sullied by their overhead equipment.

**In equally dreary** weather, Derby Corporation Roe-bodied Sunbeam F4A trolleybus No.237, built only in 1960, heads on route 60 for Derby Market Place, where several bus and trolleybus routes converged or terminated. Note how the trolleybus traction standards double as street lighting columns, and also how brackets are also used to support the trolleybus overhead. By pure chance, No.237 survives in preservation today.

**Seen in an** equally wet Derby bus station is a Felix Bus Services of Stanley, Ilkeston, Yeates Europa C41F dual-purpose bodied Bedford SB1 (618 KRA), which was new in 1959. It is operating their service from Derby to Ilkeston, which had been established in 1922, and would last until 2011. This is a good example of a small independent bus and coach operator which survived all the hazards and upheavals of war, nationalisation and deregulation of bus services.

**Also at Derby** bus station, a 1958 73-seat Willowbrookbodied Leyland PD3/4 No.421 (LRC 455) of Trent Motor Traction awaits departure on their trunk route 8 for Nottingham. Note the unusual blind-box; a type more usually associated with Ribble. Behind is one of their new Alexander-bodied Daimler Fleetlines. Trent, a BET fleet, was based in Derby and thus the major interurban operator. Recent years has seen Trent combined with the well-known independent Barton of Chilwell.

**At Derby's Market** Place terminus, Derby Corporation's 1952 Willowbrook-bodied Sunbeam F4 trolleybus No.223 has returned to the town centre, and contrasts with their 1960 Roe-bodied Sunbeam F4A No.241. Although the latter looks much more modern, all will perish just five months later!

**Also at the** Market Place we find Derby Corporation No.120, one of ten Daimler CVG6s with Park Royal bodywork new in 1957, which lasted until 1973. On this basis, the two types of Derby trolleybuses seen above should have survived until at least 1968 and 1976 respectively – more likely longer, as trolleybuses usually lasted longer than motorbuses.

**This interesting scene** at Derby Market Place sees 1960 Roe-bodied Sunbeam F4A trolleybus No.237, which we saw heading for this terminus earlier, being taken off the wires to allow one of the earlier Willowbrook-bodied Sunbeam F4 to circumnavigate the turning loop. Meanwhile, No.154, the last of ten Roe-bodied Daimler CVG6s supplied in 1963, is nearest the camera, and a similar bus brings up the rear.

**Two of Derby** Corporation's older motor buses are parked outside the depot. No.79 and No.41 are both Brush-bodied Daimler CVD6s built new in 1949 as two separate batches of five and ten respectively. These two were withdrawn in 1968, but two of these ancient-looking vehicles would survive as late as 1970, again making a mockery of the early demise of Derby's much newer and modern-looking trolleybuses.

**Of the same** type as the ones shown in the previous picture, Derby Corporation Willowbrook-bodied Sunbeam F4 trolleybus No.234, seen in the corporation's Depot, dates from 1953. To the left is No.241, another of the eight Sunbeam F4As with Roe bodies, built only in 1960. Sadly, as mentioned previously, the Corporation's trolleybus network was abandoned in September 1967. Fortunately, one of each of these types of Derby vehicles survives in preservation today.

**Back in London** again, RTL1422, one of the twenty-three examples of this class fitted with early RT10 roofbox bodies upon last overhaul in 1964, arrives at Islington, Angel early on the morning of Saturday, 8 April 1967, when I was on my way to Paddington to catch a train to South Wales. It is working trolleybus replacement route 277 from Clapton Garage, which at the time was the last to have an all-RTL allocation. RTs would gradually replace them during the last four months of the year – and seven years later I would be working as a conductor from the garage, though not on the 277, which was by then one-person-operated since the previous January.

**Encouraged by what** we saw bus-wise on our trip to Barry on Easter Sunday, Ken Wright and I returned to the area two weeks later to visit Cardiff Corporation on Saturday, 8 April 1967. On the way, we broke our journey at Newport, which had a very varied and interesting corporation bus fleet. Here, passing the historic Newport Castle, their 1949 Guy Arab III No.8, with a Guy body built on Park Royal frames, heads 1957 Longwell Greenbodied Daimler CVG6 No.160 across the road junction. The latter's body also was built on Park Royal frames, and the corporation had quite a number of their buses bodied by this company in the 1950s and 1960s. At this time, Newport was technically in England, since it was part of Monmouthshire. However, upon local government reorganisation on 1 April 1974, the town became part of the new Welsh county of Gwent.

**This strange-looking** vehicle, Newport Corporation No.37, seen in the bus station, is a unique Dennis Lancet with full-fronted D.J.Davies 38-seat bodywork, the only one with a front vertical engine. Despite its antique appearance, it was built only in 1954, but withdrawn later in 1967. D.J.Davies was based in Merthyr Tydfil, and once again the body is constructed on Park Royal frames. Davies also was a coach operator in its own right.

**Even odder is** this Newport Corporation 1956 Dennis Lancet UF single-decker, No.44 (LDW 502), also bodied by D.J. Davies on Park Royal frames, which although having an underfloor engine has a (just visible) rear open platform. Despite this, it seated forty-two passengers; a similar number to those carried on normal front-entrance single-deckers. Eight had the rear entrance, and as with the standard frontentrance vehicles all were conductor operated.

**Also at Newport** Bus Station that day, we see No.11 (UWO 498) of the tiny Bedwas & Machen Urban District Council fleet, which was the smallest municipal bus fleet in Britain with only seven buses! It is a low-bridge Massey-bodied AEC Regent V built in 1959 and, in common with the other buses owned by the council of this tiny Monmouthshire coal-mining village, passed to the new Rhymney Valley District Council on 1 April 1974.

**This view, looking** down on Newport Bus Station, shows an interesting variety of Newport Corporation buses, with 1956 Guy Arab IV No.148 nearest the camera. Once again, it has unusual bodywork – by D.J. Davies on Park Royal frames.

**No.149, another Newport** Corporation 1956 Guy Arab IV with similar D.J. Davies bodywork, undergoes heavy body repairs in the Corporation's depot. One of their more modern Alexander-bodied Leyland Atlanteans stands beside it.

**Yet another unusual** Newport Corporation bus is Longwell Green-bodied Leyland Titan PD2/40 No.177, dating from 1958 and also with Park Royal frames, which accompanies a later example of the same type, 1961-built No.68, outside the depot. Note the difference in application of the corporation's dark green and cream livery between the two. Their body manufacturer was based in a suburb of Bristol with the same name.

**From Newport, we** travelled by bus towards Cardiff, one of whose bus and trolleybus depots was on the main Newport Road right on our route anyway, on the eastern outskirts of the city. A very strange vehicle to be seen in the depot is the City Corporation's Welfare Department's Bedford SBG coach AUH 123B, which despite having a 1964 registration, carries a mid-1950s Burlingham Seagull body! It was in fact new to Goode of West Bromwich in November 1955 as SOP442, but for some reason was re-registered after acquisition by Cardiff Corporation in May 1964, and also rebuilt with a rear tail-lift. Sadly, it was destroyed by fire in 1971.

**Our main target** for that day's visit to South Wales was the Cardiff trolleybus system. Here, outside their Newport Road Depot we see 1950 Bruce-bodied BUT 9611T No.274 and 1948 East Lancs-bodied BUT 9641T No.220. I always preferred six-wheeled trolleybuses, as they reminded me of those I had known as a youngster at home in North London!

**Cardiff Corporation also** had a good variety of motorbuses. One of their last half-cabs, 1965 East Lancs/Neepsend-bodied Guy Arab V No.435 leaves the Newport Road depot to take up service, passing an older double-decker, minus engine, awaiting disposal. The large building behind them is a power station fuelled by locally-mined South Wales coal.

**We had the** pleasure of riding by trolleybus into Cardiff City Centre, revisiting the bus station outside Cardiff General Station, which we had briefly called at two weeks before. Here we find corporation trolleybus No.279, an East Lancsbodied BUT9641T built only in 1955. Some of this batch survived until the closure of Cardiff's trolleybus system in January 1970, but could have lasted a lot longer! Routes 10B, on which this one is working, and route 10A, were the last to operate them.

As we saw earlier, Western Welsh was the main interurban operator serving Cardiff, and here on 8 April 1967 we find their 1966 Marshall dualpurpose-bodied Leyland Tiger Cub single-decker No.1379 arriving at the bus station on limited stop route 301 from Neath and Bridgend. A similar vehicle in their dark red bus livery may also be seen. In common with many Western Welsh vehicles, they ended their days with National Welsh, a National Bus Company subsidiary that also took over such fleets as Red & White and United Welsh.

Rhondda was another BET subsidiary whose buses ran into Cardiff. Here, also in the bus station, is their 1957 Weymannbodied front entrance 70-seat AEC Regent V No.434 on route 120 bound for Treorchy. Note the offside illuminated advert panel, a feature popular on double-deckers in the late 1950s and 1960s, and perpetuated into the present century on some London Routemasters! Following its absorption by the National Bus Company, Rhondda was merged with Western Welsh in 1971, this operator was in turn merged later on with former Tilling Group fleets Red & White and United Welsh to form National Welsh.

**Seen at Cardiff** Corporation's Sloper Road Depot, elderly Bruce-bodied Bristol KSW 6G, No.131 was supplied to them in 1949, before Bristol chassis were restricted to being manufactured only for nationalised fleets that came under the British Transport Commission's control. It has probably been used as an extra to take supporters to Cardiff City's football ground.

**West Monmouthshire Omnibus** Traction Board 1961 Weymannbodied Leyland Tiger Cub No.3 is a stranger parked inside the depot, perhaps having taken supporters to nearby Cardiff City's Ninian Park football ground? This operator, which included such South Wales valley areas as Bedwellty and Mynyddislwyn urban districts, was renamed Islwyn Borough Transport upon local government re-organisation in 1974, which in turn finally sold out to Stagecoach in 2010.

**Looking smart outside** the depot is Cardiff Corporation No.359 (SGK 359), an East Lancs-bodied 1959 Daimler CVG6, which appears to have recently been overhauled. The peculiar-looking Bedford vehicle beside it is a tower wagon, used to service the trolleybus overhead, and also, perhaps, the corporation's street lighting columns.

**In contrast, also** at Sloper Road, No.78 (CKG 582), a 1944 wartime Bristol K6A with Park Royal bodywork (heavily rebuilt by the corporation in 1951), had been relegated to driver training duties in 1961, as so many old buses have been over the years. It remained in such use until December 1967.

**Although Cardiff Corporation** was one of few British operators to have single-deck trolleybuses, they had only a few single-deck motorbuses. One of these is No.143, a Leyland Tiger Cub with unusual Longwell Green Coachworks Ltd bodywork, one of four supplied in 1957.

**Cardiff Corporation No.213** (DBO 473), a 1948 East Lancs-bodied BUT 9641T trolleybus, still looks quite smart when on route 8 from Royal Oak to Victoria Park, via Canton and the Newport Road. Interestingly, London trolleybuses also served places called Royal Oak and Victoria Park, on routes 662/664 and 677 respectively.

**One of Cardiff's** 1955 East Lancs-bodied BUT9641T trolleybuses, No.283, is well loaded as it passes near Cardiff Castle on route 10B. As with those in Derby, these splendid vehicles should have lasted much longer than they actually did!

**Back on route** 8, earlier BUT9641T No.230, one of twenty built in 1948, again with East Lancs bodywork, is pursued by one of Cardiff's Daimler motor buses.

**Caerphilly Urban District** Council was another municipal operator whose buses ran into Cardiff. Here, under the wires, we find their early post-war all-Leyland Titan PD2/12 No.2 on a route linking Cardiff with Caerphilly. This was one of three which were new in 1951.

**A last look** at Cardiff's trolleybuses, two of which are seen on routes 3 and 1 respectively in the city centre. No.255 is nearest the camera, and is a Bruce-bodied BUT9641T new in 1949. This trolleybus system was unusual in that it was not introduced, replacing Cardiff's trams, until 1942 – at the height of the Second World War, at a time when London's tram to trolleybus conversion programme was in abeyance due to the war, never to be completed after it.

**Despite my long** day out to South Wales, the next day, Sunday, 9 April 1967, saw me attend an enthusiasts' tour to various bus and coach operators in Lincolnshire and Cambridgeshire. Here, outside the depot of the well-known independent operator Whippet of Hilton, is former London Transport RLH38 (MXX 238). This had been a Country Area bus in green livery, but looks just as smart in Whippet's dark blue. It had been sold by London Transport in September 1965, having been made redundant when normal-height double-deckers were permitted on busy route 410.

**I cannot now** remember whether the tour was another Omnibus Touring Circle one, or one organised by member Martin Haywood. The fact that we travelled on a coach owned by the famous North London independent operator Birch Brothers suggests the latter, since fellow OTC member George Ledger worked for them, and arranged the coach hire for such outings. The vehicle is K24 (KHM 24D), a 1966 Bedford VAL fitted with a Duple Vega Major body. It stands outside The Prince of Wales public house adjacent to Whippet's Hilton depot ... I did not drink in those days, though.

**Another of Whippet's** fleet seen that day is ex-Ribble 1949 Brush-bodied Leyland Titan PD2/3 Titan CCK 665. Originally No.2689 in their fleet and withdrawn in December 1960, it retains Ribble's distinctive blind arrangement, as we saw previously on the Trent Leyland PD3 in Derby. It is parked on waste ground opposite their Hilton depot, perhaps out of use, though was not officially withdrawn until September 1967.

**Eastern Counties was** another operator we visited on 9 April 1967. In their Peterborough depot we see their 1949 ECW highbridge-bodied Bristol K5G LKH429, which had recently been renumbered from LKH116. With their red and cream colour scheme and gold fleet-names and stocknumbers, this Tilling Group operator's buses were in a very similar livery to that of London Transport Central Area buses and, in fact, the whole of this batch of Bristol Ks was loaned to LT when new to help with their vehicle shortages after the Second World War, spending the year of 1949 in London and not working for Eastern Counties until the spring of 1950. This one was withdrawn in 1968.

**The vast majority** of Eastern Counties' Bristol K, KS and KSW types carried highbridge ECW bodies. This one, LKH245, is interesting in that is a K5G originally built with a wartime utility body in 1945, but given a new ECW body in 1953. The body is 8ft wide, but mounted on a 7ft 6in-wide chassis, which may be clearly seen by the positioning of the wheels and the gap between them and the outer edge of the mudguards.

**In the 1950s** and 1960s, Eastern Counties was a typical BTC and Tilling Group operator, standardising on Bristol chassis and Eastern Coach Works (ECW) bodies – the latter company in fact being based in their territory at Lowestoft. Here, also at Peterborough, their RE650 represents one of the latest vehicles from those manufacturers, being a newly delivered ECW 46-seat rear-engined Bristol RESL. Such new, one-man operated single-deckers were replacing elderly Bristol Ks like the one seen above at this period.

**In Peterborough city** centre, 1949 high-bridge Bristol K5G/ECW LKH132, another that had spent its first year on loan to London Transport, is seen on local route 303, heading for Park Farm Estate. At this period, several new housing estates were being built on the outskirts of the city, along with new light industrial estates.

**Another of the** many interesting independent operators in East Anglia was Canham of Whittlesey, which we also visited on 9 April 1967. In their depot, we find two elderly ECW highbridge-bodied Bristol Ks. On the left is LHY 948, formerly Bristol Omnibus Company No.3783 dating from 1950, and on the right GVF 74, which had been Eastern Counties' LKH74, new in the same year. Note how the former Bristol Omnibus K has bars on the outside of its front upper-deck windows. Are they meant to keep the schoolchildren it carries in, or to keep offending tree branches out? I presume the latter!

**An older ECW-bodied** doubledecker with Canham's is GPW 352, a Leyland Titan PD1A with 53-seat low-bridge bodywork, which was originally Eastern Counties AP352, new in 1947. After the nationalisation of ECW the following year, their bodies were only usually supplied to Bristol chassis until the late 1960s, as mentioned earlier. Ironically, some of their last products were fitted to Leyland chassis in the mid-1980s.

**Another elderly vehicle** seen that day is smart little Duple Vista-bodied Bedford OB JP 8139. These little 29-seaters were still fairly common with small independent operators in 1967. Its blind reads 'Load of Mischief', which implies that it was used on school contracts! It was new in 1950 to Lamb's Coaches of Upholland.

**In complete contrast,** another small vehicle seen that day is TUH 14, a 30-seat Harrington-bodied Albion Nimbus, which had been new to Western Welsh in 1960, but as remarked on earlier with the picture of one of these still with that operator, these were quickly sold on to various independent fleets when the private car began to poach traffic from buses in the Welsh valleys! It is seen with C.J. Smith's Bluebell Coaches of March, Cambridgeshire, who had acquired it in September 1966, and would sell it in April 1968.

**Former Trent 1953** all-Leyland PD2/12 No.1240 (DRC 940) is seen at the March depot of C.J. Smith's Bluebell Coaches. The rear-platform doors are of note.

**With the same** operator is PPW 861, a 37-seat Duple Vega-bodied Bedford SBO new in 1954. This had been new to Eastern Counties as their BV861, one of a batch of eighteen, which were unusual in not being the standard Bristol/ECW combination usually supplied to BTC fleets at the time.

**Pictured at the** terminus of Eastern Counties route 349 at the Market Place in March is their LC502, the first of a production batch of seventy-seven front-engined Bristol SC4LK's with 35-seat ECW bodies supplied to them between 1956 and 1961. They also had a prototype SC, which was LC501 built in 1955. These little single-deckers were ideal for rural services in the flat countryside of Fenland and other parts of East Anglia.

**Now on the** way out were older Eastern Counties single-deckers like LL712, one of four rear-entrance 35-seat ECW-bodied Bristol L5G's built in 1950. It too is seen in March. One of this batch, LL710, as well as LL718, one of the twenty-three longer Bristol 39-seat LL5Gs supplied in 1950/51, is smartly preserved at the East Anglia Transport Museum at Carlton Colville, near Lowestoft.

**Driven out for** photographs outside Eastern Counties' March depot, their LL744 is an experimental Bristol LS4X, with Gardiner 4LW engine and ECW 41-seat bodywork. The hundreds of standard Bristol LS's delivered to BTC fleets throughout the country in the early/mid-1950s derived from this vehicle, but did not perpetuate its frowning appearance! It is hard to believe that this was built alongside antique-looking half-cab Bristol L-types as seen above! This important prototype happily survives today. Having been secured for preservation after its withdrawal in April 1972, it is in the care of Ipswich Transport Museum.

**Of similar vintage,** former London Transport MCWbodied AEC Regal IV RF282 (MLL 819) is now No.177 in the fleet of the famous Cambridgeshire independent Premier Travel, one of several redundant Green Line coaches acquired in 1964/65. It is seen in Cambridge bus station. Ironically, at this same period, many of the survivors of this batch in London were being modernised and saw as many as eleven more years on Green Line work.

**Seen also in** Cambridge that day is RE649, another of Eastern Counties' brand new ECW-bodied Bristol RESL single-deckers.

**Back in London,** the final batch of 160 RML-class 72-seat Routemasters was now entering service. These replaced the smaller 64-seat RMs which, in turn, replaced the fast dwindling number of RTLs directly, or RTs, which, in turn, were moved on to replace RTLs. At this point, I decided to try to photograph every surviving RTL, of which some 400 or so of the original 1,631 remained in service, and did manage to do so! I was aided in this by having exact records showing when they were last overhauled, so went for those that had been done longest ago first, since the usual criteria for their withdrawal was when their certificates of fitness expired and they would need another overhaul. This one, RTL1368 is another of the twenty-three RTLs fitted with early roof-box RT10 bodies (i.e. those whose mountings were modified to fit either RT or RTL chassis and which were hitherto fitted to RTs) upon overhaul in 1964. This was done to allow newer bodies then fitted to RTLs to be overhauled and out-shopped on RT chassis, which were expected to last longer, as indeed they did. Only four other RTLs had ever had roofbox bodies, including the first one (RTL501) and three others overhauled with them in the mid/late 1950s, all of which had been withdrawn by the time the 1964 examples appeared. RTL1368, seen on Lambeth Bridge on 10 April 1967, is working tram replacement route 168 from Stockwell Garage, which will begin to receive RTs to replace RTLs on this route, and the 77A/C, a few weeks later.

**At Victoria, RTL1031,** due for imminent withdrawal having last been overhauled in the spring of 1962, is one of two standing outside Gillingham Street Garage whilst on loan there from nearby Battersea for route 137 to cover for a shortage of Routemasters. Gillingham Street's own allocation of RTLs for route 10 had been withdrawn at the end of 1966, whilst that on the 137 had been replaced by RM's in the autumn of 1964, as had those on route 52 two years later. This garage was built new in 1939 with ground-level accommodation for buses and a basement intended to house Green Line coaches, many of which terminated at nearby Eccleston Bridge. Owing to the war, this latter proposal was never fulfilled. Instead, the basement was used to house service vehicles and, when their own premises across the road were demolished to make way for construction of the new Victoria Line tube, Post Office vans. Later on, coaches used on overnight services from Scotland and the North East to Victoria Coach Station spent their daytime layover period there, and finally some of Gillingham Street's 'Red Arrow' single-deckers and 'midi-buses' were housed there. The garage was closed in 1993.

**At Lambeth Palace** on route 10, about to cross the bridge, RTL559 is one of only three of the 450 Metro Cammell-bodied RTLs still in service. They were all at Bow Garage and were withdrawn shortly after this picture was taken. London's route 10, which once ran all the way from Victoria to Abridge, Essex via London Bridge, Aldgate, Bow, Stratford and Woodford, was converted to the awful DMS class of one-man-operated double-deckers in October 1972. This hastened its demise – it no longer exists today; the present route 10 was introduced in 1988, running from Kings Cross to Hammersmith, having nothing at all in common with the original.

**For several years,** Willesden Garage had a Saturday allocation on route 18, which had been extended and converted to RM operation to replace trolleybus route 662 on 3 January 1962. At first RTWs were used, but following their demise at that garage in the spring of 1965, RTLs were operated. Here, on 15 April 1967, their RTL1506 passes The Prince Of Wales public house in Harrow Road en-route to Sudbury. This was one of the 100 RTLs overhauled during the latter part of 1965, when overhauling them had to be resumed due to delays in production of new buses for London meant to replace them. This did not, however, save them, as all were withdrawn by the end of November 1968, when Willesden Garage was the last to operate RTLs. This allocation, though, was withdrawn on 7 September that year. Note the trolleybus traction standard still in use for street lighting on the right of this picture, more than five years after the last trolleybuses ran along the Harrow Road.

**I rode on route** 18, whether on an RTL or not I no longer recall, that day to Wembley, where an England v Scotland football match was on. Of course, my reason for being there was the coaches the event brought, one of which is the splendid 1965 Alexander-bodied AEC Reliance EUS 10C, with the Scottish Co-Operative Wholesale Society of Glasgow, who used the fleetname 'Majestic'. In 1967, the only Alexander-bodied vehicles to be seen in London were coaches such as this, usually on overnight services to and from Scotland – today, there are hundreds, if not thousands, of them working London's bus services!

**Much of my** leave from my work for the Greater London Council at County Hall in the spring of 1967 was spent pursuing RTLs. Here on 19 April 1967, Battersea RTL1233 approaches Holborn Station on route 22, which converted to RM operation in May. It is pursued by an RM on route 23, which apparently has attracted the attention of the Point Inspector seen on the right, whilst one of Maidstone & District's Harrington-bodied AEC Reliance coaches heads in the other direction.

**RTL1628 is another** Battersea bus, seen the same day in Regent Street on route 39, which then ran from Southfields to Finsbury Park, with a rush hour extension to Tottenham Garage. At this time, Battersea Garage was gradually receiving RTs, some of which were overhauled red ex-green, being former Country Area or Green Line vehicles, to replace its RTLs on routes 19, 22, 31 and 39. This latter route was the only one of the four never to receive RMs – it converted to the awful DMS type in July 1972, and had been also withdrawn north of Oxford Circus in January 1970.

**From Regent Street,** I travelled on an RML on route 15 to Limehouse, where we find Poplar RTL1568 leaving the route 56 terminus for a trip around the Isle of Dogs loop to Blackwall Tunnel. Like RTL1628 above, it had not entered service until March 1958, having been surplus to requirements when built in late 1954. Both had just one Aldenham overhaul, early in 1962, and carried bodies that had also only been in use since early 1958. Despite this, both were withdrawn shortly after these pictures were taken. Route 56, which had served the Isle of Dogs for many years, was also withdrawn in October 1969 and replaced by an extension of route 277 from Cubitt Town to Poplar. Today, much of that area has changed unrecognisably, with the regeneration of Docklands and the creation of the International Finance centre around Canary Wharf.

**Another Poplar bus** which will soon be withdrawn is RTL452, which has just emerged from the 'new' Blackwall Tunnel on its way from Crystal Palace to Bromley-by-Bow on 'tunnel' route 108. At this time, the new tunnel – intended as the southbound one – was in use for traffic in both directions, whilst the roadway in the old, original one (to become the northbound one) was being widened. This was done not by breaking out the original pavements in it, but by the cheaper option of filling in the space between them to widen the roadway which, however, caused it to be too low for double-deck buses!

**The former tram** and trolleybus depot at Poplar was used for many years as a store for withdrawn vehicles, which often outnumbered its own, fairly small working allocation! This was so on 19 April 1967. Seen gathering dust here are RTW477, which had latterly been in use as a trainer, Metro Cammellbodied RTL703 and RTL627, and standard RTL391. This view clearly shows how the standard RTL on the right has a thicker waistband than the two others, and the RTW. The RTW also immediately looks wider than the RTLs – which it was, but only by 6 inches! The 500 RTWs had similar Leyland Titan PD2 chassis to the RTLs, but were also bodied by Leyland. Many withdrawn vehicles stored here were sold for further use in Ceylon and South Africa, the garage being handy for exporting them from the nearby docks.

**There was also** a bus route through the Rotherhithe Tunnel at this period, the 82 also operated by Poplar RTLs. RTL1215 (LYF 156) emerges from the tunnel on its way to the nearby terminus at Stepney East station (now renamed Limehouse) on 19 April 1967. RTs replaced the RTLs on this route as well as the 108 and 108A upon 'reshaping' on 7 September 1968, but lasted only until the end of October, when the 82 was withdrawn without replacement, and the 108 converted to single-deck. The 108A retained doubledeckers but was cut back to Greenwich, thus avoiding the tunnel. Today, no bus route runs through the Rotherhithe Tunnel.

**My journey homewards** to Canonbury that day took me on an RML on route 5 to Old Street station, where we see Clapton RTL1335 (MXX 34) in the evening rush hour on route 253A. This route had been introduced in February 1964, following trolleybus replacement route 253 from Finsbury Park to Cambridge Heath, and then route 170 to Bloomsbury. The RTLs were gradually replaced by RTs in the last four months of 1967. The route was withdrawn in March 1968. Very strangely, this RTL had travelled to Czechoslovakia a few months previously, yet returned to service at Clapton – only to be withdrawn a few weeks later.

**Although London Transport's** garages at Hackney, Bow, Poplar and West Ham are often perceived as being the last stronghold of the RTL class, this was in fact in north-west London at Stonebridge Park, Willesden and Cricklewood garages. At the latter on 22 April 1967, RTL1152 (LYF 92) and RTL1320 (MLL 682) have arrived at the garage, RTL1152 from route 2, which it had operated for many years, and on which buses ran 'dead' to and from Childs Hill.

**On the evening** of the same day, one of Southdown's Northern Counties full-fronted Leyland Titan PD3s, No.315 (GUF 250D) dating from 1966, has brought a party of theatregoers to London, and has been parked at Bressenden Place, Victoria. The last batches of these vehicles had the 'panoramic' windows seen here, which were viewed by many (including me) as being ugly, and a far cry from the graceful 'Queen Mary' PD3s of earlier years.

**Another 'theatre' coach** at Bressenden Place that evening is Boon's of Boreham, Essex Duple Vista-bodied Bedford OB (PTW 268), which had been new to Stacey's Coaches of Little Baddow in 1950. It is in front of a more recent Duple-bodied coach.

**On Sunday, 23 April** 1967, I was on yet another enthusiasts' tour to the well-known independent operator Provincial, otherwise known at Gosport & Fareham. This operator was renowned for its 'antique' buses, many of which were heavily rebuilt, or re-bodied, to keep them in service. Here at their Hoeford depot are two pre-war Harrington-bodied AEC Regal 4s. Nearest the camera is CG9607, which when I took this I had no idea it would — many years later — be preserved and attending bus rallies I have been involved in organising at North Weald and Theydon Bois. It was new in 1934, but the body was substantially rebuilt in 1962. At the time of writing it is still going strong at the age of eighty.

**Also illustrating how** heavily rebuilt some of Provincial's buses were, their No.17, a wartime Guy Arab II new in 1945 with a Park Royal utility body, was given this new, full-fronted Reading body in 1957.

**A more conventional** Guy Arab in the Provincial fleet, No.31 was new in 1943 as a wartime utility vehicle to Cheltenham & District, but taken over by Red & White in 1946. They renumbered it L1943, and it was re-bodied by Brislington Body Works (BBW) in the early 1950s. It had recently been acquired by Provincial when seen here.

**Inside Provincial's Hoeford** depot, in contrast to the other buses seen above, venerable Park Royal-bodied AEC Regent I FHO 602 was new to them in 1935, and was still going strong in largely unaltered condition thirty-two years later! Similar Regent BOR 767 is splendidly preserved today, by David Whittaker of Waltham Abbey, who is also proud owner of Regal IV CG9607.

**The last major** London trunk route serving the City and West End to be fully RTL-operated was route 25, running from Victoria to Becontree Heath via Oxford Circus, Holborn, Aldgate, Stratford and Ilford. It was operated by Bow and West Ham Garages, who would lose them amid the first stage of London Transport's ill-fated 'Reshaping Plan' on 7 September 1968. That is all in the future as Bow RTL1420 on a short working to Aldgate escorts two others through the city along Leadenhall Street on 27 April 1967. In more recent times, route 25 suffered the ignominy of being operated by 'Bendibuses', and today runs only from Tottenham Court Road to Ilford, though at least has double-deckers again.

**Next day, Friday,** 28 April 1967, Stockwell-based RTL1170 (LYF 111) loads up in Vauxhall Bridge Road, Victoria, bound for Crystal Palace on route 2. Having worked 'short' from the south, it waits on the bus stand. A few days later, this RTL was withdrawn when RMs displaced elsewhere by new RMLs were 'cascaded' (to use a twenty-first century term) to routes 2 and 2A at Cricklewood and Stockwell garages.

**A second or** so after photographing the RTL in the previous picture, which may be seen in the background here, I was turned to stone when the prototype rear-engined, front entrance Routemaster, FRM1, suddenly appeared in Vauxhall Bridge Road, having apparently been in nearby Gillingham Street Garage whilst on a test run. As may be seen it is running on trade plates, and far as I am aware, this was the first time this somewhat 'hush-hush' vehicle had been photographed in public, as it did not appear at the 1966 Commercial Motor Show as had been intended. Completed in 1966, it was to have been one of four prototypes for a new generation of such vehicles, but probably owing to the severe financial restraints this country was by then facing, Barbara Castle, the Minister of Transport, forced London Transport to abandon the policy of buying buses built to its own designs. In future they would have to operate 'off-the-peg' designs from bus manufacturers instead, resulting in the disastrous MB, SM and DMS types purchased between 1967 and 1978. This was most unfortunate, because if a fleet of rear-engined Routemaster buses, presumably manufactured by AEC, Park Royal and perhaps Leyland, suitable for one-man operation, had been built, they could have lasted at least into the present century, as many traditional RM-types did in London anyway, and all the disasters of the 1970s would have been avoided! As it was, the FRM's body was clearly a progression of the existing Routemaster design, and as may be seen, at first it had non-opening windows and forced air ventilation. This was not, however, a success. The bus entered service in July 1967 on routes 34B and 76 from Tottenham Garage, for evaluation trials alongside the XA-class Leyland Atlanteans (see earlier in this book), but suffered an engine fire in December of that year. When repaired, it was fitted with opening windows of the same quarter-drop type as fitted to RM's and RML's. Meanwhile FRM1 remained at Tottenham until late in 1969, then moving to Croydon and later Potters Bar for use as a one-man-operated bus on local, outer-0suburban services. After that it was used on the Round London Sightseeing Tour, before becoming part of the London Transport Museum collection. It is still active today, showing 'what might have been' and returned to route 76 for a special run on the route's centenary in July 2013.

**This view of** FRM1 turning from Gillingham Street into Vauxhall Bridge Road shows its unique rear end. The upper-deck rear emergency exit window is identical to that on a standard Routemaster; the shrouded rear engine is in similar style to the Daimler Fleetlines and Leyland Atlanteans of the era. It is worth noting that the latter type had first appeared in 1958, the same year that London's first 'production' Routemaster, with conventional front engine and open-rear platform, was built!

**Two more mundane** London Transport buses are seen in Battersea Bridge Road later the same day. Nearest the camera, Saunders roofbox-bodied RT4819 is arriving, also on trade plates, at Battersea Garage, where it will be re-licensed on 1 May to replace RTLs, one of which, RTL360, changes crew behind it on route 39. Such was London Transport's determination to get rid of the surviving RTLs at this time that roofbox Saunders-bodied RTs which had bodies up to five years older than those carried by some RTLs were used to replace them. There were 300 RTs with this make of body, built at Beaumaris on the island of Anglesey by the Saunders Engineering & Shipyard Company to a similar design to the majority of RTs whose bodies were built by Park Royal and Weymann. Built between 1949 and 1951, they were the last London buses to feature the roof route-number box, which had first appeared in the 1920s. Most survived to receive a last overhaul in 1965/66. The final Saunders vehicle was withdrawn in March 1971, by coincidence at Battersea Garage.

Saturday, 29 April 1967 saw me travel west again by train from Paddington, but only as far as Reading, whose corporation still had a sizeable trolleybus fleet. Pride of place went to a batch of twelve Sunbeams with H.V. Burlingham Ltd 68-seat forward-entrance bodies built only in the summer of 1961 to replace earlier vehicles. Here, No.189 turns at Broad Street in the town centre.

Also in the town centre, No.187 of the same batch heads for Wokingham Road on route 17. Note the forward entrance, which could have made these splendid trolleybuses suitable for one-man operation.

**Thames Valley was** the main inter-urban operator serving Reading, and here a group of their vehicles – all standard Tilling Group ECW bodied Bristols in their red and cream livery – stand outside what was then called Reading General Station. No.775 nearest the camera has recently been transferred from United Welsh. It was new as their No.1256 in 1955, and is a Bristol LD6B Lodekka. Three later Lodekkas of the FLF variety are on the right and behind it; at the extreme left, an older Bristol KSW may be seen.

**A look inside** Thames Valley's Reading Depot shows a variety of ECW-bodied Bristol LS single-deckers. On the left, S313 was originally a coach in the associated South Midland fleet, and has recently been downgraded to dual-purpose status. In the centre, S325 is an ex-United Welsh vehicle, delivered new as No.1255 in 1955. Similar LS bus S683 on the right was new as such to Thames Valley.

**Seen lined up** with some of its fellows in Reading Corporation's Mill Lane trolleybus depot is their No.177, one of twelve Sunbeam six wheelers with 68-seat Park Royal bodies built in 1950. They carried a dark maroon livery, with cream relief bands.

**Also at the** depot is No.140, a 56-seat BUT four-wheeler, also with Park Royal bodywork. Twenty of these were delivered to Reading Corporation in 1949.

**No.189 a 1961**
Sunbeam trolleybus with a Burlingham body, in Reading town centre. Sadly, this system was abandoned in November 1968, but some of this batch of trolleybuses saw further service on Teesside, which was the penultimate British trolleybus system to close, in April 1971.

**Of the same** batch, Reading trolleybus No.185 climbs out of town on route 15, bound for Northumberland Ave. Note how the overhead is supported by crossbars between the traction standards.

**Smith's of Reading** was a well-known independent operator, which not only had luxury coaches for touring and private hire, but also second-hand buses from major operators used for school and industrial contracts. Here at their depot are recently acquired ex-South Wales Transport Nos.442 (MCY 402) and 460 Weymann Orion-bodied AEC Regent Vs. Both were built only in 1955/56, so hopefully they are to be refurbished for further use rather than cannibalised for spare parts.

**More typical of** Smith's fleet is their Duple Vega-bodied Bedford SB RRD 330, new in 1958, seen in the company of a group of other Duple-bodied coaches.

**An unusual coach** seen parked at Waterloo the same evening is JHL 670, a Plaxton-bodied Atkinson CPL 745H dating from 1956, and new to Halcyon Coaches of Hull. Here, it is operated by Kirby's Coaches of Bushey, who had acquired it in May 1960. The coach park was opposite the Old Vic Theatre in Waterloo Road. Today, a public open space and children's playground occupy the site.

**Even stranger is** HMR 444, a Plaxton-bodied Leyland Royal Tiger new in 1951 to Typhoon Coaches of Westbury. It had been lengthened by Sparshatt of Portsmouth to the newly permitted length for British buses and coaches of 36ft, as allowed from 1962 onwards, and operated later on by Horlock's Coaches of Northfleet, Kent. Here, it is unusually parked in the forecourt of Charing Cross Station collecting a private party when seen on 1 May 1967 working for President Coaches. Even more remarkably, this coach received a new Plaxton body in 1971, when it was also re-registered!

**Of similar vintage,** Green Line coach RF43 is seen heading for Reigate on cross-London route 711 at Piccadilly Circus on the same day. By now, most of these vehicles still used as Green Line coaches had been modernised, and this was one of the last to remain in original 1951 condition. It was modernised shortly after this picture was taken, and was later preserved.

**At this period,** I travelled on most Saturdays down the London & South Western main line from Waterloo to film and photograph steam trains in their last weeks of working at such places as Basingstoke or Woking. With a group of friends, I usually caught the 7.18am from Waterloo to spend much of the day at the lineside. This involved leaving the station and finding a spot further on down the line, so I was also able to photograph any local buses I saw on the way. Here at Woking on 6 May 1967, Aldershot & District Alexander-bodied Dennis Loline III No.445, one of twenty built in 1962, has just passed beneath the main line at Woking Station heading for Guildford on route 29.

**In common with** fellow BET operator East Kent, as mentioned previously, Aldershot & District standardised on AEC vehicles for their single-deck and coach fleets once Dennis had ended full-size single-deck production in the mid-1950s. Here, also at Woking, Aldershot & District No.543 has an interesting pedigree, being one of twenty-five AEC Reliance coaches new in 1954 with unusual Strachan centre-entrance bodies. Originally No.250 in this batch, it was one of fifteen withdrawn in 1965 and given brand new Metro Cammell bus bodies early in 1967, and has recently re-entered service in this form when seen here at Aldershot & District's depot.

**Woking was one** of several 'border towns' on the edge of the London Transport area, where their Country Area buses (and sometimes, Central Area ones too, as in Slough and Brentwood) mingled with those of provincial operators – in this case Aldershot & District. Here, RLH25, one of seventy-six AEC Regent IIIs with Weymann low-bridge bodies built in 1950 and 1952 heads for Ripley on route 436A. As mentioned previously, the first twenty of this class were a diverted order from Midland General; this is one of the second batch which were actually ordered by London Transport. The last Country Area survivors, at Guildford and Addlestone, lasted until the end of July 1970, needed owing to the plethora of low railway bridges in this area. By coincidence, their bodies were built in Addlestone too, as Weymann's factory was located in the town.

**Back in my** home area, RTL1003 is seen in Essex Road, Islington, running back to Clapton Garage in the evening rush hour of 8 May 1967 on trolleybus replacement route 277. Interestingly, the destination 'Hackney Station' was shown for buses terminating there, despite the fact that the station was closed during the war, and not reopened (as Hackney Central) until 1980! By then, all RTLs were long gone, this one perishing shortly after this picture was taken. A Saunders-bodied RT running in to Leyton Garage on route 38A follows, whilst an RM on route 73 heads in the opposite direction.

**A favourite spot** for me to photograph buses in the years when I 'worked' at County Hall was Parliament Square, just across Westminster Bridge. Here on 10 May 1967, Saunders roofbox-bodied RT4352 from Elmers End Garage works the long route 12, which ran all the way from South Croydon to Harlesden, Willesden Junction, albeit usually in overlapping sections. No fewer than four garages worked it at this period – South Croydon, Elmers End, Rye Lane (Peckham) and Shepherd's Bush. It would convert to Routemaster operation in the spring of 1973.

**Passing my place** of employment, County Hall, on 10 May 1967, Clapton RTL1331 also heads for home, alias 'Hackney Station', on tram and trolleybus replacement route 170. Note its adverts for London Transports 'New Weekender Tickets' on the front. These were excellent value for money, covering all of London Transports' Central Area and most Country Area routes, Green Line coaches and the Underground on Saturdays and Sundays, or Sundays and Bank Holiday Mondays. The side advert still shows Red Rover tickets at six shillings each (30p), which they had been since early 1962 – and would be until June 1968, again excellent value!

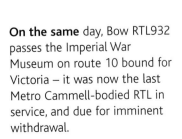

**On the same** day, Bow RTL932 passes the Imperial War Museum on route 10 bound for Victoria – it was now the last Metro Cammell-bodied RTL in service, and due for imminent withdrawal.

**By this time,** half-cab coaches and single-deck buses were becoming quite a rarity, but here at Lambeth Palace also on 10 May 1967, is CDY 408, a Thomas Harrington & Sons Ltd-bodied AEC Regal new in 1946, whose bodywork recalls the designs of the late 1930s. New to Skinner's Coaches of St Leonards, it passed in 1951 to the fleet of Gilbert's Coaches of Tunbridge Wells, one of whose Bedford OBs we saw earlier. This operator was renowned for keeping elderly coaches going in the 1960s, but sold this one on to British Rail a few weeks after this picture was taken.

**At the same** spot we see former London Transport RTL1256, working as nurses' transport for nearby St Thomas's Hospital with Albert Harling. In a smart dark green and cream livery, it is one of the eighteen RTLs overhauled by LT for use at Hatfield Garage in 1959, the only members of the class ever to run in Lincoln green Country Area livery. Because they were more sluggish in steering than the RTs crews were used to, staff at Hatfield disliked them and they were soon demoted to training duties. This one was 'de-roofed' in a low bridge accident, but Harling's bought and repaired it themselves, using the roof and windows (the parts painted cream) from a scrap RT with identical bodywork! Today, it is smartly preserved by Imperial Coachways of Harlow, restored to 1959 Country Area livery and it occasionally may even be seen in service on special occasions. Unlike RTL1323, which was also preserved and fraudulently painted in Green Line livery for many years, this one is the genuine item and the only survivor of the ill-fated green RTLs.

**On 21 May** 1967, I travelled on an OTC trip to Sheffield. This was the first time I had ever visited Yorkshire, which could now be reached on a day trip by coach from London thanks to a recent extension further north of the M1 Motorway! Alas, nearly all of the photographs I took that day were ruined by the firm who developed them! Sheffield Corporation 1955 M.C.W.-bodied AEC Regent III No.354 is seen in a very wet and windswept city centre, with the awful Park Hill Estate perched on the hill behind. At the time it was seen as an emblem of 1960s 'progress'.

**Next day, 22** May 1967, I was at London Transports Poplar Garage again. In the centre of this large, cavernous ex-London County Council tram depot, Poplar's roofbox RTL1438 has run in from Rotherhithe Tunnel route 82, probably on a 'spreadover' duty, where buses and crews worked in the morning and evening rush hours, with a long break (for which crews were paid!) in between. On the left may be seen some of the many withdrawn RTLs and RTWs stored there, which often outnumbered Poplar's service buses. This was particularly so on the night of 6/7 September 1968, when all 200 or so RTLs in the East End perished, and many were sent there for storage.

**On 23 May** 1967, the bridge over the North London Line in Highbury Grove was closed due to emergency repairs, and buses on routes 4A and 19 had to be diverted via St Paul's Road, Canonbury Station and Grosvenor Avenue. Here, RT10 roof-box bodied RT2243 from Holloway Garage is about to turn from Grosvenor Avenue back to its correct route in Highbury Grove on the 4A. The body carried by this RT, classified RT10, is identical to that carried by the RTL in the previous photograph; the only visual difference between them is the different radiators, for this AEC Regent RT, and the Leyland Titan PD2 RTL. Bodies between the two types were exchanged upon overhaul at London Transport's Aldenham Works. Such was the high degree of standardisation achieved by London Transport in the 1950s and 1960s. On the left of the bus may be seen Highbury County Grammar School, which I attended between 1959 and 1964. The original Victorian buildings were about to be demolished, new buildings on the former playground may be seen behind them. In September 1967, these opened as the new Highbury Grove Comprehensive School, echoing the Wilson government's education policies of the time.

**Caught passing my** original home in Canonbury Avenue the same day, local operator Cream Coaches of Islington's 1955 Duple Bodies & Motors Ltd Vega-bodied Bedford SB RLM593 is seen on hire to London Transport for the rail replacement service on the Northern City Line tube between Moorgate and Finsbury Park. This resulted from the diversion of its northbound tunnel at nearby Highbury & Islington Station to afford cross-platform interchange with the new Victoria Line.

**776AOO is a** strange-looking little coach, built in 1963 with bodywork by Thurgood of Ware, and Ford 530E chassis. Seen near Willesden Junction Station on 25 May 1967, it is with Parker's Coaches of Harlesden, who had acquired it at the end of 1964 from its original operator, Super Coaches of Upminster. Super was the forerunner of today's very successful Ensignbus.

**Passing the famous** Jubilee Clock in Harlesden, which was once rounded by London's graceful trolleybuses on routes 660, 662, 664 and 666, DFA 550 is a 1955 AEC Reliance with Willowbrook dual-purpose bodywork, which had been new to Victoria Coaches of Woodville, and is now working for a contractor.

**London Transport's RTLs** and RTWs, as well as Leyland-engined RMs, which had the same Leyland O600 engines, were renowned for their loud engine notes, and here Willesden RTL1589 roars along Pound Lane, near its home garage, on route 226. Note its 'lazy' via blind, which, however, is incorrectly shown as it is intended for short workings on this route, whereas the bus is actually working throughout from Golders Green to Harlesden, and then further on to its rush hour extension to Park Royal, where buses terminated adjacent to the factory where many RT and RTL bodies had been built, as well as all production Routemasters, which were still being produced there at this time. This RTL is one of those overhauled as extras in the latter part of 1965, and survived until the end of RTL operation in London on 29 November 1968, when Willesden's routes 176 and 226 were the very last to operate them.

**Another mid-1950s** coach seen with a contractor that day is Duple-bodied Leyland Royal Tiger PSU1/16 NCD 665, which has just passed beneath the Midland main line at Cricklewood Station. New to Southdown as their No.1665 in March 1954, it had recently been sold to John Laing Construction.

**This busy scene** in Kilburn High Road, also on 25 May 1967, finds Cricklewood RTL1259 on weekday route 60 bound for Colindale escorting an RM from the same garage on route 16. These two routes paralleled each other all the way along the Edgware Road from just north of Cricklewood to Marble Arch, but whereas route 16 had been one of the first to gain Routemasters to replace RT-types, at the end of 1962, route 60 was never allocated them. Instead it was withdrawn on 7 September 1968 and partly replaced by new RMoperated route 8B.

**RTL137 changes crew** on 26 May 1967 outside Clapton Garage, where as mentioned earlier I would be working myself as a conductor seven years later. At this period, the garage worked route 106, which ran all the way from Finsbury Park to Becontree, to where this one is bound. Clapton lost this allocation in March 1968, by which time RTs had replaced RTLs on the 106 which, in turn, was cut back to Blackwall Tunnel in January 1971. Today it only runs from Finsbury Park to Whitechapel.

**Shortly before withdrawal,** Cricklewood RTL1557 stands at Edgware Station awaiting departure for Golders Green on route 240 on 11 July 1967. After sale, this RTL was sold to a film company, appearing in several films, notably the Hammer horror films *Quatermass And The Pit* and *Son Of Jack The Ripper*. It gained most fame when supposedly being burnt out in an episode of the TV series *On the Buses* in 1973. Beside the RTL is RM977 on route 221, which had been extended from North Finchley to Edgware in 1966, replacing parts of routes 125 and 240A.

**On 11 July 1967,** an extremely rare working on trolleybus replacement route 266 is that of Stonebridge Park RTL1599 (OLD 819), seen heading north from Cricklewood Broadway on a short working to West Hendon. This route had always been RM operated, but Stonebridge Park had a small allocation of RTLs for route 112, from which this one has strayed on to it.

**Midland Red had** for many years built their own buses and coaches, and in 1950 built twelve 26-seat touring coaches, classified C2, which originally had Duple-built bodies. However, in the mid-1960s, these were re-bodied with new Plaxton bodies. One of them, No.3346, is seen here at Marble Arch, pressed into use on one of their Associated Motorways express services to Victoria.

**Earlier, we saw** an RTL on a former trolleybus replacement route, and here we see Walthamstow RT2707 at Clapton Pond on 14 July 1967 on another, route 257. This too was a very rare working: the 257 had also always been RM operated, and remained so until withdrawal on 7 September 1968. Walthamstow had acquired RTs for routes 34 and 144 in 1964, initially to cover while Leyton Garage was being rebuilt, but in fact retained them until these routes were converted to one-person-operation (OPO) in September 1977 and January 1974 respectively. This one has strayed onto route 257, perhaps owing to a shortage of RMs at the garage.

**Back on OTC** tours, one on 6 August 1967 again took us to East Anglia, including the well-known independent Delaine of Bourne, Lincs. Here, their brand new Duple Vega Major-bodied Bedford VAL No.62 (GTL 825E) is proudly driven out for the photographers. With their smart dark blue livery, Delaine's buses and coaches are still going strong today.

**Delaine often favoured** bodywork by Yeates of Loughborough. Here is their No.47 (MTL 750), a Yeates Europa-bodied Leyland Tiger Cub PSUC1/2, built to dual-purpose specification, i.e. for use either on bus or coachwork.

**Once an important** market town on the Great North Road, Stamford, was by-passed by the Great Northern Railway's main line, and subsequently declined in importance. However in 1967, it was served by three Tilling Group companies – Eastern Counties, Lincolnshire and United Counties. Here in the bus station is the latter's No.491, a standard 41-seat ECW-bodied Bristol LS6B new in 1954.

**With similar-looking** bodywork to the coach sold to Laing's that we saw earlier, No.1053 (RUF 53) is still in use with Southdown when seen at Victoria on 15 August 1967, but in fact has a Beadle body mounted on the newer Leyland Tiger Cub PSUC1/2 chassis. It was new in May 1956, and withdrawn in 1968. By coincidence, it too was sold to a contractor, in this case Wimpey Construction. On the left, one of the Alexander-bodied coaches used on overnight services to Scotland loads up with passengers' luggage.

**In contrast, most** of London Transport's Green Line RFs dating from 1951/52 were given a new lease of life at this period. Seen at Addington Street, Waterloo, on 4 September 1967, RF176 heading for Reigate on route 711 has recently been done, but seems almost empty in this lunchtime view! By now, once important cross-London Green Line coach routes like this were being affected by increasing traffic congestion, and also competition from improved commuter train services. In many cases, they were divided into two sections and terminated in Central London or, in the case of the 711, withdrawn completely a few years later.

**Seen on the** same day, Maidstone & District 1958 Harrington Wayfarer-bodied AEC Reliance coach C388 is parked outside the Palace of Westminster, presumably on a touring trip. These coaches also ran express services between Victoria and the Medway towns.

**I have purposely** included only one image of a standard London Transport Routemaster in this book, having published several books dedicated to them in past years. Here, RM461 (WLT 461) has just been transferred to New Cross Garage to replace RTs on route 53 after being displaced by new RMLs on route 207 at Hanwell Garage.

**One of my** favourite operators outside London was Birmingham City Transport, many of whose buses were built with similarly-styled bodies on different chassis, contemporary and similar to how London's RT, RTL and RTW buses were. However this one, No.296, is a standard all-Leyland Titan PD2 – being in fact one of the prototypes of that famous type, delivered in 1947, and withdrawn shortly after this picture was taken. It has been driven out for us on yet another OTC tour, on 10 August 1967, at Birmingham's Hockley Garage. This had originally been a tram depot.

**Also at Hockley** is No.2139, one of the fifty 'production batch' all-Leyland Titan PD2s delivered to Birmingham in 1949. The last of this batch, including this one, were withdrawn in 1968. Note the tram tracks still in place beneath it, despite their having been replaced by buses here in 1939!

**A further fifty** Leyland Titan PD2s were delivered to Birmingham in 1949/50, but with Park Royal bodywork, built alongside London's RTLs, which had similar chassis. However, these buses seated only fifty-four as opposed to the standard fifty-six in London. This is No.2183 (JOJ 139), also seen at Hockley. It, too, was withdrawn in 1968, with the last survivors of the batch withdrawn in 1969.

**With the style** of bodywork and tin-front radiator typical of Birmingham buses in the early 1950s, No.2663 is a Metro Cammell-bodied Daimer CVD6, one of 150 delivered in 1951. It was withdrawn in 1969. As with most London Transport trolleybuses and RMtypes (as well as later OMO buses), those in Birmingham had matching registration and stock-numbers for more than thirty years. In fact, the whole of the registration block JOJ1-999 was used for them. The fact that Birmingham City Council was also the licensing authority no doubt helped!

**Of the same** batch as the previous vehicle, Birmingham No.2760 poses for us at Rosebery Street Garage. This, too, was a former tram depot, converted to bus operation in 1947. This vehicle, unlike No.2663, was one of several of its batch to pass to West Midlands PTE when that entity took over the Birmingham, Walsall, West Bromwich and Wolverhampton municipal fleets in October 1969

**Birmingham's Perry Barr** Garage was built new in 1932, and usually referred to by crews as 'Wellhead Lane', which buses showed on their blinds when terminating there. That is so in this view of No.1707, one of a hundred Brush 54-seat Leyland Titan PD2s built in 1948. It has an earlier style of standard Birmingham bodywork, similar to that seen on the Coventry vehicles earlier in this book. This one was one of the last survivors of its batch, withdrawn in 1968.

**MetroCammell-bodied** Daimler CVG6 No.1845, also seen at Perry Barr Garage, is one of a batch of eighty-seven delivered in 1948/49, with almost identical bodywork to the Brush-bodied Leyland PD2 seen above. Almost 300 similarly-bodied Daimler CVD6's were also delivered to Birmingham between 1948 and 1951. Withdrawal had already begun when this photograph was taken, and this vehicle was withdrawn in 1968 – as were all of the others by the end of that year.

**At the same** location is No.2245, one of thirty MCW 34-seat forward-entrance Leyland Tiger PS2s built in 1950. Along with five rare Leyland Olympics built at the same time, these were Birmingham's only singledeckers for many years, until a batch of twenty-four very unusual Daimler Fleetline with Marshall single-deck bodies arrived in 1965. Remarkably, though, three of these Tigers survived to be taken over by West Midlands PTE in 1969!

**The grand finale** of the OTCs 1967 season was a weekend trip to Blackpool for the illuminated trams on the weekend of 9 September 1967. Reaching Altrincham on the Friday evening, and staying there, we called at various interesting operators on the Saturday, spent Saturday night in Blackpool, then called at other operators on our way back to London on Sunday. Our first port of call was Warrington Corporation, whose No.24, a 1946 all-Leyland Titan PD1, has now been demoted to training duties.

**Another elderly Warrington** vehicle is No.97, one of three Guy Arab 6LW single-deckers built in 1948/9 with 33-seat forward entrance Guy bodywork. By now, such vehicles were very rare indeed in municipal service!

**Another Guy seen** that day is at Birkenhead Corporation, our next port of call. Also demoted to training duties, their No.193 is a Guy Arab III with Massey bodywork, one of fifteen new in 1950. It had been demoted to training duties in 1965; the last of this batch were withdrawn from passenger service in 1966.

**Behind it stands** No.266, one of five Leyland Titan PD2/12s new in 1954 with unusual Ashcroft bodywork, built in Widnes. It would survive to be included in Merseyside PTEs absorption of Birkenhead Corporation in 1969.

**A second municipal** operator on the Wirral peninsula was Wallasey Corporation, which we also visited. No.69 is one of eleven Weymann-bodied Leyland Titan PD2/12s built in 1951, and was withdrawn in 1968, though some of the batch survived to pass to Merseyside PTE when Wallasey's fleet too was absorbed into it in 1969. Note the peculiar livery, officially described as 'sea green and cream', though the 'sea green' looks more like yellow!

**Another Wallasey bus,** No.43 has an unusual history, its chassis being a Leyland Titan PD2/10 built in 1957. However its antiquated-looking Metro-Cammell body was new in 1951 to the original No.43 (AHF 839) whose PD2/1 chassis was destroyed in 1959! Even more curiously, the chassis of the original No.43 had been new as No.8 with a second-hand 1948 Burlingham half-cab coach body originally fitted to a 1936 Leyland TD4 double-decker. The result seen here, rather like the famous 'hammer with two new heads and three new handles', actually survived to pass to Merseyside PTE, too.

**On into Lancashire,** we visited the Atherton depot and works of the famous independent operator Lancashire United Transport, where we see No.90, a Weymann low bridge-bodied Leyland Titan TD4 new in 1940, converted to open-top for tree lopping after withdrawal in 1957.

**Also at Atherton** is Lancashire United No.593, last of twenty-four Weymann Orion-bodied Daimler CVG6s new in 1956. Note the power station chimney with the company's 'LUT' initials on the left, a relic of the former South Lancashire trams and trolleybuses, which LUT had inherited. At the time of our visit, LUT was the largest British independent bus fleet, and it worked closely with the various small municipal fleets in the area. However, it was eventually taken over by Greater Manchester PTE, finally ceasing operation as an independent entity in 1981.

**One of the** many small Lancashire municipal fleets mentioned above was Widnes Corporation, whose depot we also visited that day. A remarkable relic to greet us was this ancient Leyland Lion single-decker, used as a towing vehicle. It is No.69, one of three type LT7 Lions, with Massey bodywork, new in 1935. Luckily, having been retained so long as a towing vehicle, it has survived into preservation, being in the care of the North West Museum of Road Transport.

**More modern is** Widnes Corporation No.15 the last of nine all-Leyland Titan PD2/1s built for them between 1948 and 1950. Note its unusual upper deck front windows, one of which opens and the other not, giving a 'winking' effect! The operator was renamed Halton Transport in April 1974. Sister bus No.14 stands next to it.

**Wigan Corporation was** next on our list. Here at their depot is No.101, a 43-seat Northern Counties-bodied Leyland Royal Tiger new in 1953. This operator would become part of the South East Lancashire and North East Cheshire PTE. (SELNEC for short!) in 1969.

**At our destination,** Blackpool tram No.304 passes an ornate seafront public convenience on its way to Fleetwood. At this period, Blackpool was the only British operator to retain trams, which by now were more of a seafront attraction than anything else. This one is the first of a batch of twenty-five centre-entrance single-deckers built by Charles Roberts between 1952 and 1954.

**Heading in the** opposite direction is car No.311 of the same batch. The forbidding looking 'castle' in the background is in fact the Norbreck Hydro Hotel, where we stayed that Saturday evening. By coincidence, my father had been stationed there briefly during the war when the building was taken over by the army.

**On our way** back south on Sunday, 10 September 1967, we called at Preston Corporation's depot, where their all-Leyland Titan PD1 94 is posed for us, one of a batch of nineteen supplied in 1946/47, and now due for early withdrawal.

**A more modern** Leyland Titan is No.30 one of eighteen PD2/10s built for Preston in 1957 and unusually carrying Crossley bodywork. This very much resembled Park Royal products of the period. The bus appears to have been recently repainted in the corporation's maroon and cream livery, with its coat of arms clearly shown below the lower-deck windows.

**In contrast to** the two Leyland Titans seen earlier in Preston Corporation's traditional maroon livery, No.81 has been painted in an experimental livery of light blue and white as part of a trial to choose a new livery. With this style, the crest almost disappears into the blue panels. It is one of five PD2/10 built in 1955 with Metro-Cammell Orion bodies.

**A second Preston** Leyland Titan PD2/10 in an experimental livery, this time a darker blue and white, is No.43, one of thirteen built between 1952 and 1954 with Leyland bodywork. We were all asked which version we preferred. I preferred the darker version seen here. Notably, the crest is given a white background, so stands out more clearly. Eventually, a blue and cream colour scheme was adopted in the 1970s. Following English bus service deregulation (outside London) in 1986, the corporation's fleet and services were subject to a 'management buy-out', becoming Preston Bus.

**One of the** smallest Lancashire municipal operators was Leigh Corporation, which was our last port of call on the way back to London. No.7 is one of eighteen lowbridge Leyland Titan PD2/3's built in 1949/50, and one of twelve, very unusually for this area, bodied by Lydney. The other six had Roberts bodywork. This one was withdrawn in 1969, shortly before Leigh's fleet was absorbed by SELNEC, to which a few of the batch survived to be allocated.

**Another unusual Leigh** Corporation double-decker is No.33, a lowbridge Roberts-bodied AEC Regent III also dating from 1949. AECs were rare in what was effectively Leyland's home territory, especially with municipal fleets. This one was the last survivor of a batch of ten, withdrawn a few weeks after our visit. The coach seen behind it is Birch Brothers 1964 Harrington Cavalier-bodied AEC Reliance K25, which had taken us on our weekend outing to Blackpool.

**Leigh Corporation's East** Lancs-bodied Leyland Tiger Cub No.2 is more typical of buses to be found in the area, one of two supplied in 1959, which were their only single-deckers. Both survived to be taken over by SELNEC. I remember one of our party delighted in having the destination 'Infirmary' shown on its blind which, so he said, was appropriate for at least one of us who had drunk too much on the Saturday night and was literally green in the face next morning … no, it wasn't me!

**We saw earlier** one of West Riding's Roe-bodied Guy Wulfrunians in Wakefield, bearing their standard green and cream livery, in Bradford early on the morning of Saturday, 7 October 1967. At the same time and location is No.977 in their red and cream livery, which was carried by buses which had replaced Wakefield's trams on local services back in the 1920s. Its crew sit on the pavement enjoying a fag before setting off.

**No.737 of** the same batch changes crew outside the depot. This one lasted until the end, and is now one of several Bradford trolleybuses that survive in preservation.

**My main purpose** in travelling to South Yorkshire with a couple of friends that morning, by overnight train from Kings Cross, was to visit the trolleybuses in Bradford. We broke our journey at Wakefield to visit the engine shed, which had recently been closed but still held several dozen withdrawn steam engines. Our first port of call in Bradford was Thornbury Depot, outside which trolleybus No.729 had just suffered a spectacular dewirement under the web of overhead. It is a Karrier W new to Bradford Corporation in 1946, and given a new East Lancs front-entrance body in 1959. It survived until 1971, by which time Bradford was Britain's last trolleybus operator.

**With similar East** Lancs bodywork, though with a rear entrance, Bradford trolleybus No.588 was new to the Notts & Derby system in 1941, and bought by Bradford Corporation when that system closed in 1953. It is an AEC 664T originally with Weymann bodywork, and was re-bodied by East Lancs in 1958, remaining in service in that form for ten years. It is seen near Forster Square station.

**At the same** location is No.788, another trolleybus rebodied with a forward-entrance East Lancs body. It is a Karrier W, new to Darlington Corporation in 1944 originally with a singledeck Brush body. Acquired by Bradford in 1957, it was rebodied in 1958 and lasted in service until 1971. Several others of the batch were acquired by Bradford for spares only.

**As will be** clear by now, not only was Bradford the last British trolleybus operator, but the corporation also bought trolleybuses from several other operators when they discarded them. No.777, seen also near Forster Square Station, came from Llanelly whose system was abandoned following takeover by South Wales Transport in 1953. New in 1945, it was one of ten Karrier W's Bradford acquired from them as chassis only, and once again had been rebodied by East Lancs, in rear-entrance configuration. This one lasted until 1971.

**Bradford's most modern** trolleybuses were five East Lancs-bodied BUT9611Ts, which had been new to Darlington Corporation in 1949, but sold to Doncaster Corporation only three years later in 1952. In turn, Doncaster sold them to Bradford in 1960, curiously three years before their own system closed. They were given new East Lancs forward-entrance bodies in 1962, and here we see No.834 climbing out of Bradford city centre bound for Buttershaw. None lasted until the end, however, all were withdrawn in 1971.

**On the same** route, No.794 shows that not all the trolleybuses acquired by Bradford Corporation received new bodies. It is one of eight BUT 9611Ts with East Lancs bodywork new to St Helen's Corporation in 1951. They were acquired by Bradford in 1958, and rebuilt by Roe. Two of them survived until 1971, but this one perished in 1968.

**A few trolleybuses** supplied new to Bradford retained their original bodies, too. No.753 is a Weymann-bodied BUT 9611T, one of four delivered in 1950. The other three were withdrawn in 1964, but this one soldiered on until 1970, and so I was lucky to catch this picture as in 1967 it was the only survivor already.

**On Sunday, 8** October 1967, the splendidly preserved London Transport C2-class AEC trolleybus No.260 did a tour of the Reading system, and despite my very long day visiting Bradford the day before, I travelled west to see it. Here it has arrived at Reading General Station.

**Also under the** wires outside Reading General Station, ex-London Transport RTW467 (LLU 957) has carried a group of enthusiasts, perhaps members of the fledgling LOTS for which it ran outings in those days, to see No.260 back on the wires. This RTW had been the last at London's service, from Brixton Garage in May 1966, and went into private preservation soon after. However, RTWs never operated London's route 10 in real life! It was still an RTL stronghold at the time.

**An oddity seen** at Smith's of Reading's depot the same day is NRA 717, an early post-war Crossley SD42/7 single-decker, with Crossley bodywork, new to Chesterfield Corporation in 1949, and now apparently used by a local college. Withdrawn in November 1965, it was later preserved, and though it ended up being cannibalised for spares in the mid-1980s, two others of the batch survive.

**For some reason,** Reading Corporation No.138, the first of twenty Park Royal-bodied BUT 9611T trolleybuses built in 1949, is parked outside Mill Lane depot with booms down. At least this batch had a reasonably long life in their hometown, whose system closed in November 1968, unlike Reading's splendid Burlingham-bodied Sunbeams, new only in the summer of 1961!

**About 35 miles** west of London trolleybus route 626's real terminus, No.260 heads for home (by then in Edmonton Garage) after a tremendously successful day under Reading's wires. It is hard to believe that this splendid vehicle, which had served routes in north-west London from 1936 to 1959, was originally selected by London Transport as a museum exhibit, but discarded in 1961 in favour of a similar-looking all-Leyland K type. Fortunately, a group of enthusiasts, not least Tony Belton and Fred Ivey, saved the vehicle.

**I end this** volume of photographs with this view of London Transport RT10 roof-box bodied RTL1383 working from West Ham Garage at the Victoria Station terminus of route 25 in the evening rush hour of 29 November 1967. Little did I know then that exactly a year later, London's last RTLs would be withdrawn from service. Although several hundred were exported overseas for further use, mainly in Ceylon (Sri-Lanka), and hundreds more went for scrap, a few survive in preservation today, some in working order.

## Part Three

# A BRIEF LOOK AT THE BUS ENTHUSIAST MOVEMENT

nterest in buses runs along similar lines, no pun intended, to that in railways and their operation. The enthusiast can be merely the humble 'spotter', wanting to see every bus or coach owned and operated by a certain fleet, or indeed every fleet, carefully keeping record of which vehicles he has seen, or someone who keeps a record of the routes they operate, their chassis types and makes, the bodies they carry, their destination indicator blinds, the different garages and depots they operate from, and so on. He may also collect the tickets issued on the buses or the maps and timetables detailing their routes or, as is more relevant to this publication, photograph the vehicles. My own interest in buses, as mentioned in this book's introduction, included all of these things, sparked by the replacement of my local trams, and then trolleybuses, by motor buses in the 1950s. This interest can then progress further, to preserving old buses and coaches, to running societies dedicated to the hobby and to organising rallies and so on to display them, as well as to producing films and books on the subject. Once again, my own interest has progressed in this way over the years.

Bus enthusiasts are in a minority when compared to the better-known railway enthusiasts (which I also am), but the history of the bus enthusiast movement in Britain goes back a long way. One of the earliest official groups dedicated to the subject is The Omnibus Society, whose members began to collate data on bus and coach operation, relating to the vehicles themselves and the services they operated, along with the histories of the fleets that operated them, back in the 1920s. Then, during the Second World War, the PSV Circle was founded. This group too, initially in London, began to keep detailed records of where buses were garaged, when they were overhauled and what routes they operated, as well as how these routes changed. The bus scene was a fascinating one when this group started up, some seventy years ago, with such unfortunate incidents as German flying bombs wrecking bus garages and trolleybus depots (i.e. Elmers End, Bexleyheath and West Ham) and all of the vehicles in them. In those days, photography was very difficult, not only with shortages of the necessary photographic materials, but also with the threat of being arrested as a German spy.

In tandem with that in railways, the hobby blossomed in the very early post-war years, not least thanks to Ian Allan, who had published his ABC booklets listing and detailing railway locomotives actually during the war, and then produced similar ones on buses, coaches, trams and trolleybuses

**Early former Eastern** Counties Leyland Titan DR4902 arrives at Brighton having taken part in the May 1967 London to Brighton Historic Commercial Vehicle Cub run.

immediately after it. The hobby of 'spotting' (i.e. collecting their numbers) had existed to a limited extent before the war, but these publications gave it the boost it needed to become a national pastime, mainly for youngsters but also for the 'not so young' in the early post-war years and through into the 1960s. The same publisher also produced magazines on both subjects (*Trains Illustrated* and *Buses Illustrated*). The latter first appeared about eighteen months after I was born. More than anything else, the early post-war years were a time of tremendous change to Britain's buses and railways not only with the onset of nationalisation, but also with the replacement of war-weary and worn out vehicles and rolling stock with long-overdue new ones. Wartime developments in technology accelerated this pace of change, with new types of engine and of vehicle construction being made available for civilian use. Most noteworthy, perhaps, was the appearance of the first mass-produced underfloor engined single decker buses and coaches, which would soon oust most of the earlier types with their traditional half-cabs and front engines. The abandonment of Britain's tramway systems, which had begun well before the war, continued, but after the war, motorbuses rather than trolleybuses replaced them, and then the trolleybuses were replaced by motorbuses. That too was of tremendous interest to enthusiasts, the older of whom strove to record everything possible of the doomed trams and trolleybuses, whilst the younger 'spotter' enthusiasts tended to be more attracted by the shiny new buses, particularly the thousands of new RT-types and then the new Routemasters in London, which replaced them.

The Omnibus Society also published a magazine for its members, who were generally older and more 'serious' enthusiasts, whilst the PSV Circle produced monthly newsletters, detailing latest developments – new buses, sales of old ones, changes of garage allocation, details of bus overhauls and changes to routes. Soon, just as Ian Allan's

ABC booklets covered bus operators up and down the country, the PSV Circle's newsletters covered different areas of the country, each usually with its own editors in the relevant areas. Naturally, too, both the Ominbus Society and the PSV Circle organised meetings for their members in various parts of the country. I remember how at first, only older enthusiasts were allowed to join them. I had to get special dispensation to join both groups, at the age of sixteen early in 1964. Clearly, by then, they did not want humble 'bus spotters'. By that time my own interest had already progressed to photographing the vehicles and, for London Transport, keeping exact records of their allocations and overhaul details. So, on the strength of that, they accepted me. Both societies are still going strong today.

As the 1950s and 1960s progressed, other enthusiast groups began to emerge, often specialising either in preserving historic vehicles, or in recording precise details of all aspects of bus operation by a particular operator. In the latter instance, the London Omnibus Traction Society (LOTS, as it is generally known today) came into being fifty years ago, dedicated to London Transport's huge bus and coach fleet. Today it is the country's biggest bus enthusiasts' society, still keeping and publishing details of bus operators and their vehicles and routes in the area that London Transport once served, approximately to a radius of about 40 miles around London. Forty-five years ago, I compiled for them the first complete, current list to be published of the numbers of bodies carried by each of the 8,000 or so London Transport buses then in that operator's fleet. This was particularly important since most London buses exchanged bodies when overhauled at London Transport's famous Aldenham overhaul works, and the document was published to coincide with the split between London's Central Area (red) buses and County Area (green) buses at the end of 1969, and formed a basis upon which subsequent records of overhauls, as published by both LOTS and the PSV Circle, could be built. I am still proud of it forty-five years later.

By this time, the bus preservation movement was getting under way, though was still in its infancy. Initially, several operators had had the foresight to preserve some of their historic vehicles after they had been withdrawn from public service. London Transport (and indeed its predecessor London General) had done very well in this, and by the early 1960s, several of these, along with a few historic buses from other operators and, most incongruously, various historic locomotives (not least Sir Nigel Gresley's famous, world-beating *Mallard*), were displayed in the Museum of British Transport – in reality a redundant London Transport bus garage and former tram depot in Clapham High Street. Subsequently, London Transport set up its own museum, and although the main building in Covent Garden that still exists today caters more for London's tourists, with such things as taxicabs being displayed as well as historic buses, trams and Underground trains, enthusiasts are catered for by a much larger display of London's historic buses and coaches, along with railway rolling stock and artefacts in the museum's 'Acton Depot', adjacent to the London Underground's Ealing Common depot. It is, however, only usually open on special occasions.

Fortunately, many other operators – notably municipal fleets who had usually operated trams and trolleybuses – also kept historic vehicles from their bygone fleets, displaying them in museums in their hometown.

By 1967, the year in which my photographs in this book were taken, amateur preservationists were coming to the fore. For some years, the Historic Commercial Vehicle Club (HCVC) had organised a road run from London to Brighton, culminating in a display of the historic vehicles along the seafront. Although the 'official' run at that time, which included such vehicles as vans, lorries and fire engines as well as buses and coaches, was somewhat 'exclusive', there were always of course 'hangers on' tagging along behind them

on the road run, often by 1967 a procession of recently withdrawn former London Transport RT types. Also at this period, the Crich Tramway Museum in Derbyshire had been set up. This was particularly important since, other than in Blackpool, no full-size trams ran anywhere in Britain by then. Once again, this museum is still in operation today, with a stretch of track on which a variety of trams which once graced the streets of various British towns and cities run to re-create what once was a commonplace sight throughout the country.

As already mentioned in the main body of this book, the Omnibus Touring Circle, an offshoot of the PSV Circle, organised monthly outings for bus enthusiasts in the 1960s. Not only were visits arranged to such attractions as the Brighton HCVC Rally or the Crich Tramway Museum, but also to individual bus and coach operators, usually those close enough to be reached within a day from London. The ever-expanding motorway network in the 1960s enabled such outings to reach as far as Yorkshire by the time we got to 1967, whilst there was also usually a weekend outing taking in the Blackpool illuminations (in which their trams featured) that visited bus operators in the north-west on the way there and back again. The operators visited on these tours were always very welcoming, driving out interesting buses and coaches from their depots for us to photograph, as shown in several of my pictures in this book.

It is amusing, although perhaps sad, to recall that, in stark contrast to the well-organised OTC trips that were run by reputable, responsible people using buses or coaches owned and operated by bona-fide public service vehicle operators, the operation of such trips by the disreputable also took place back in the 1960s. This gave bus and railway enthusiasts a bad name, perhaps explaining why we are derided as 'cranks' or 'anoraks' today. Who remembers, for example, a clapped-out former London Transport bus that would turn up unannounced and uninvited outside a London Transport bus garage on a Sunday morning, disgorging a

**In this view** taken on the OTC visit to Coventry Corporation's depot on 19 March 1967, several members of the group may be seen photographing other buses in the background of this shot of Coventry's 1949 Metro-Cammell-bodied Daimler CVA6 No.69, now demoted to driver training duties. And there's not an anorak to be seen – the enthusiasts are wearing sports jackets, suits or raincoats!

rabble of twelve or 13-year-old bus spotters who would promptly invade the premises, to the horror of the garage staff. Perhaps this explains why, in the 1960s, all London Transport bus garages and trolleybus depots had notices outside them proclaiming that 'children under sixteen were not allowed on the premises in any circumstances'. Similar 'invasions' would be made at British Railways engine sheds by young train spotters and,

worst of all, sometimes items would be pilfered from these establishments. Favourites were the metal garage code plates and running numbers that London buses carried on their sides in those days, which could be easily removed and put in a coat pocket. It is noteworthy that London Transport never allowed visits to their bus garages and trolleybus depots in the 1950s and 1960s, and also very seldom organised public visits to their fascinating Aldenham and Chiswick bus overhaul works. Only in the 1970s did the spectacle of open days at their garages start to occur, and this was more in an attempt to showcase bus operation to the general public than it was for the benefit of enthusiasts. This is still the case today with their successor operators.

On the credit side, by far the great majority of amateur groups involved in keeping records of bus and coach operation and preserving historic buses and coaches grew into serious and reputable organisations that have in later years consolidated the hobby. By the early 1970s, rallies of preserved buses had begun to be organised up and down the country quite independently of the original HCVC events, whilst also, museums housing preserved vehicles began to spring up too, also independent of bus and coach operators. The one at Cobham in Surrey is a case in point.

There were also myriad individual vehicle preservation projects and as traditional types of bus and coach began to be replaced by what in the late 1960s and early 1970s were regarded as boring – standardised, one-man operated types – more and more of these older types began to be rescued for preservation. Most importantly, with the unfortunately rapid demise of British trolleybus systems in those same years, it became imperative to preserve as many of these vehicles, which had almost as diverse chassis and body makes and types as motorbuses, as possible. Such groups as the British Trolleybus Society and the National Trolleybus Association made sure that a good variety of them were preserved, along with the London Trolleybus Preservation Society dedicated to keeping London's trolleybuses alive. Today, a splendid museum dedicated to trolleybuses, many of which may be seen running under an extensive system of overhead wires, exists at Sandtoft near Doncaster, while other trolleybuses also still exist in working order, notably at the East Anglia Transport Museum at Carlton Colville near Lowestoft, where several of the London trolleybuses reside.

Just as the upkeep of preserved railway locomotives and rolling stock from bygone years can be a 'labour of love' and take up virtually unlimited amounts of time and money, so also can that of preserved buses and coaches. Particularly for individual preservationists not allied to a major transport museum (and these are perhaps in the

majority), just finding somewhere safe and secure to house the vehicles can be a major problem. You cannot merely park a doubledeck bus outside your house, as its height will obstruct your neighbours' daylight, for a start, unless you live at some remote spot out on the moors. Because the bodies on most older buses and coaches are of 'composite' construction, i.e. of wood and metal, they are prone to rot and rust, particularly if kept static, and so it is desirable for them to be kept under cover, away from the wind and rain. That is not easy with a doubledeck bus that is 14ft 6in high, and can be 8ft wide and 30ft or more long. There is also the problem of graffiti and vandalism, or worse, arson. Sadly, many has been the time – and not just recently – that owners have been heartbroken when some mindless idiot has broken in to their premises and reduced their cherished vehicles to ashes. More than once, priceless, unique examples of Britain's transport heritage have been lost in this way.

Other than museums housing, and sometimes operating, preserved historic buses, since the 1960s, the organisation of bus rallies has grown tremendously up and down the country. Some of these are run by genuine bus enthusiasts and preservations, others by professional companies, presumably for private profit rather than, as in the former category, to raise funds for the upkeep of the actual vehicles themselves or for the running costs of the preservation societies organising them. At first, such rallies were merely static displays of the vehicles, lined up for all and sundry to examine and to photograph. Sometimes there would be a 'vintage bus service' linking these rallies, often on remote former wartime airfields, with 'civilisation', i.e. the nearest railway station. Originally featuring only old, preserved vehicles, these rallies soon began to attract operational vehicles from various bus companies, who could display their latest vehicles to the public, too. A good example of this type of rally is that at North Weald, near Epping in Essex. Held on the former Second World War RAF fighter airfield

**Preserved London Transport** C2-class trolleybus No.260, is typical of those that served London so well between 1935 and 1962. Photographed on the Reading system on 8 October 1967, it was the first such vehicle to be rescued by the LTPS, and is still kept in full-working order at the East Anglia Transport Museum in Carlton Colville, near Lowestoft.

there at first in 1981 and featuring almost entirely preserved London Transport buses, this was taken over by the North London Transport Society in 1984, and soon attracted buses and coaches of virtually all shapes, types, makes and ages from all over the country, with a network of vintage bus services linking it to nearby Epping underground station and various other local towns. I was one of its main organisers until 2012, and today it is still going strong, linked with the nearby Epping Ongar steam railway with a service of historic buses, referred to in today's terms as 'heritage buses'.

Unlike some of the other bus rallies, North Weald has also raised thousands of pounds for a variety of charities (for instance the Leukaemia Research Fund, the London Transport branch of the St John Ambulance Brigade, the Royal National Lifeboat Institution and the Harlow Lions) over the years.

A further development in the display and operation of preserved buses has been that of the 'running day'. Here, various types of bus and coach are brought to areas where they once ran, in an attempt to re-create 'yesterday's transport scene'. Great care is taken to ensure the buses are in the right liveries, and that, usually, they are the correct types of vehicle to re-create the period concerned, and carry the correct destination blinds for the relevant area, that they did, in say, the 1950s. Of course, the facts that many of the buildings in the areas they run in have been built since then and that other road traffic is modern, is usually lost on those who organise and attend these events, which nevertheless are thoroughly enjoyed by everyone.

Bus memorabilia is often sold at such rallies and running days. This can range from simply photographs, films or books featuring buses and coaches (whether vintage or modern), to bus timetables, maps, tickets, destination blinds, mechanical or body parts to keep 'ancient' buses going, or even (as at larger events such as North Weald), buses themselves. And then there are the model buses. When I first started selling such memorabilia in support of a preserved steam locomotive of which I was a co-owner at such events in the early 1970s, 90 per cent at least of the goods on offer were merely books, photographs, timetables and maps. But today, model buses dominate the scene. Starting with the Dinky Toys of the 1940s and early 1950s, such models now have a life of their own, with, for instance, a model of a standard London Routemaster bus being produced in literally hundreds of different variations of livery, route blind displays and so on. Today, indoor sales catering for transport enthusiasts (both buses and railways) are big business, especially where their models are concerned.

Where will it all end? As someone who has been a bus and railway enthusiast for more than sixty years, and involved with the transport enthusiast movement for best part of fifty, I often hear it said that this is a dying hobby, as it is now generally regarded as unusual to see anyone of under fifty years of age as a serious transport enthusiast at, for instance, a bus rally. But is that really so? True, gone are the days of fifty years ago when a dozen or so enthusiasts (including me) would be encamped outside Victoria Coach Station on a summer Saturday noting and photographing the myriad different coaches arriving there, and the London Transport RTW-class buses passing by on routes 11, 39 and 46. However, as mentioned above, enthusiasts' groups such as the London Omnibus Traction Society, the Omnibus Society and the PSV Circle are still going strong. Are most of the members older

enthusiasts such as myself who like to purchase their publications which hark back to what are, to me, the happier days of the 1950s and 1960s, or are they younger people who maintain an interest in current developments in the bus industry? Of course, I should not let my judgement on this topic be clouded by the fact that I myself have little or no interest in current developments, least of all the ridiculous 'New Routemaster' bus project in London, which is squandering so much in scarce public funds for what many regard as the London Mayor's 'vanity project'. There is also the question, of course, as to whether those enthusiasts who are interested in current bus operation are also interested in Britain's transport heritage, and vice-versa. These are questions I cannot answer: The fact that there are so many websites on the internet today dedicated to our hobby suggests that it is not dead yet and that, perhaps, younger enthusiasts do exist in greater numbers than the dearth of them at bus rallies and so on implies – perhaps they indulge in their hobby via the internet?

In recent years, too, several well-established bus rallies have been discontinued, for instance those once held at Southend-On-Sea and Southsea. The main reasons for this have been vast increases in public liability insurance costs, which are obligatory at such large events, following the terrorist attacks in New York in 2001 and London in 2005, as well as ever-pervasive 'Health & Safety' regulations imposed on them, particularly if the rallies are staged on premises owned by local or public authorities. A further problem has been drastic increases in fuel costs, which have deterred owners from bringing their vehicles long distances to these events. Finally, many enthusiasts nowadays prefer to visit events such as 'running days' where they can ride on historic vehicles, usually free of charge, rather than merely to see them lined up at static rallies at which, quite often, the same vehicles may be seen year after year.

However, the operation of historic, preserved buses and coaches at 'running days' may itself be brought to an end by European Union

**A group of** bus enthusiasts compare notes and photographs at Victoria Green Line Coach Station one Easter Monday in the 1960s. Where are they now?

legislation, which from the beginning of 2017 will mean that all buses and coaches running on Britain's roads must be 'disability friendly', in other words, able to accommodate wheelchairs. Of course, this is primarily meant to refer to buses and coaches running in normal, fare-paying public service, whereas most of those at rallies and 'running days' run free services. It is certainly the case that paying 'heritage services', for example that using the surviving original London Routemaster buses on route 15, will be affected by this latest intrusion into British life by the 'Eurocrats' in Brussels, and will have to be withdrawn. At the time of writing, Transport for London's Director of Surface Transport Operation, Leon Daniels, himself a long-standing bus enthusiast and preservationist, is trying to find

some way to avoid this happening. Perhaps the answer would be to fit these few surviving original London Routemasters still at London's service with a second entrance/exit capable of handling wheelchairs? This is not as ridiculous as it sounds, since a couple of them were so adapted for the Round London Sightseeing Tour in the 1980s.

It is also worth pondering whether an interest in buses, be it from the operational point of view, or in their preservation, is a purely 'British' phenomenon. Some may think it is, especially when similar movements exist in many Commonwealth countries, for instance Canada, Australia, New Zealand and South Africa, where British-built buses once predominated, and also in the USA to where many have been exported over the years. However, many preserved buses and trams exist in Germany, notably in Berlin, where double-deck buses developed in much the same way as they did in London, and suffered even more than their London counterparts during the bombing of the Second World War. Other countries in mainland Europe have bus preservationists too, for instance Holland and Spain.

It is heartening to recall that many senior figures in Britain's bus industry are bus enthusiasts, and this has been so since at least the 1960s. At least two of the most senior figures running Transport for London are long-standing enthusiasts and more's the pity that they have had to obey the orders of London Mayors such as Ken Livingstone and Boris Johnson, rather than carry out their own policies. My old friend Paul Everett, who was with me when many of the pictures in this book were taken and who has been such a great help in checking details of them, spent more than forty years in London's bus industry, retiring as a senior manager with one of our biggest bus operators a few years ago.

Finally, every hobby has its eccentrics. Anyone who has a serious interest, as a hobby, in buses may perhaps be regarded as 'eccentric' by the average person, but for some reason this hobby (as also does that involving railways) seems for no apparent reason to attract those who, to put it kindly, may be regarded as 'ultra-eccentric'. In all the hundreds, if not thousands, of transport enthusiasts I have known since the 1950s, one person stands out as the most eccentric of all. He was literally obsessed by London's RTL-class and RTW-class buses, of which there were a total of 1,631 and 500 respectively, and he could rattle off the complete history of each bus from memory when asked. This was no mean feat, since some of them saw twenty years at London's service, working from several different garages and on many different routes. They also exchanged bodies upon overhaul as many as four times: But he knew them all, and he always got the details right. He also had literally thousands of photographs of these buses, which adorned all the walls and doors of his home. Sadly, he is no longer around on the bus enthusiast scene, he suffered a serious epileptic fit some twenty years ago and has been in hospital ever since, and perhaps still alive.